Time to Say No

Time to Say No
Alternatives to EU Membership

Ian Milne

Foreword by
Lord Vinson LVO DL

Civitas: Institute for the Study of Civil Society
London

First Published October 2011

© Civitas 2011
55 Tufton Street
London SW1P 3QL

email: books@civitas.org.uk

ISBN 978-1-906837-32-7

Independence: Civitas: Institute for the Study of Civil Society is a registered educational charity (No. 1085494) and a company limited by guarantee (No. 04023541). Civitas is financed from a variety of private sources to avoid over-reliance on any single or small group of donors.

All publications are independently refereed. All the Institute's publications seek to further its objective of promoting the advancement of learning. The views expressed are those of the authors, not of the Institute.

Typeset by
Civitas

Printed in Great Britain by

Berforts Group Ltd
Stevenage SG1 2BH

Contents

		Page
Author		vii
Summary		viii
Key to References		viii
Glossary		ix
Foreword	Lord Vinson of Roddam Dene LVO DL	xi

1 The Economics of EU Membership	1
2 Eight Reasons Why the UK Doesn't Need the EU Single Market	5
3 Sectoral Questions	8
4 Alternatives to Full EU Membership	11
5 How the UK Would Prosper after Withdrawal from the EU	15
6 The Road to Self-Government	18

Appendix

Global Britain Briefing Notes

Number

58: The Commonwealth and British Export Growth 2010 – 2050	25
59: European Union 2009 Prosperity Rankings	33
60: Eighty-eight per cent of the UK Trade Deficit over the Last Five Years was with EU-26	39
61: The EU *has* to negotiate Free Trade Agreements with Third-Parties—and It Does	44
62: A Country Doesn't Need to Belong to the EU to Trade with It	46
63: The Proper Definition of 'Trade'	49
64: The Rotterdam-Antwerp Effect and the Netherlands Distortion	53

65: The Economic Cost of EU Membership   57

66: Exports of Germany, France and the UK in 2009   61

67: Less than Ten Per Cent of the British Economy is Involved in Exporting to the EU   65

68: The Non-existent 'Benefits' of Belonging to the EU Single Market   67

69: The Coming EU Demographic Winter   70

70: EU Customs Duties   72

71: 'Keeping the Peace' in Western Europe   74

72: How EU Law is Made   76

Author

Ian Milne has been the Director of the cross-party think-tank Global Britain since 1999. He was the founder-editor (in 1993) of *The European Journal*, and the co-founder (in 1995) and first editor of *eurofacts*. He is the translator of *Europe's Road to War*, by Paul-Marie Coûteaux, and the author of numerous pamphlets, articles and book reviews, mainly about the relationship between the UK and the European Union. His most recent publications are *A Cost Too Far?* (Civitas, July 2004), an analysis of the net economic costs and benefits for the UK of EU membership; *Backing the Wrong Horse* (Centre for Policy Studies, December 2004), a review of the UK's global trading arrangements and options for the future; and *Lost Illusions: British Foreign Policy* (The Bruges Group, December 2007), which assesses UK foreign policy since 1945 and suggests how it could become more effective.

He graduated in engineering from Cambridge University and in business administration from Cranfield. His business career was in industry and merchant banking in the UK, France and Belgium.

Summary

This book contains five short papers (of around 1,000 words each):

1. The Economics of EU Membership

2. Eight Reasons Why the UK Doesn't Need the Single Market

3. Sectoral Questions

4. Alternatives to Full EU Membership

5. How the UK Would Prosper after Withdrawal from the EU

The papers overlap somewhat, and differ in style and format; but all are based on the hard facts and data set out in the Appendix.

A sixth paper, rather longer, 'The Road to Self-Government', looks forward to the summer of 2014. Unlike the preceding five, it is a work of imagination. It postulates that the British people have voted in a referendum for UK withdrawal from the EU. It consists of the letter setting out the timetable and mechanics of British withdrawal that a British Prime Minister would promptly send to EU functionaries and the leaders of EU member-countries, as well as Switzerland, EEA countries and Turkey.

The Appendix contains the texts of 15 of the most recent Global Britain Briefing Notes.

Ian Milne, Director, Global Britain
September 2011
www.globalbritain.org

Key to References

In the text, 'BNs' refer to Global Britain Briefing Notes Nos 58 to 72, which can be found in the Appendix starting on p. 25.

'BNs' with an asterisk (e.g. BN35*) are not reproduced here, but can be found at www.globalbritain.org/ briefingnotes.asp

'Wrong Horse' refers to *Backing the Wrong Horse* by Ian Milne, Centre for Policy Studies (2004), accessible at www.civitas.org.uk/wronghorse.pdf

Glossary

ACTF   *A Cost Too Far*, by Ian Milne: www.civitas.org.uk/pdf/cs37.pdf

BN   Global Britain Briefing Note
www.globalbritain.org/briefingnotes.asp

CAP   Common Agricultural Policy

CBA   Cost-Benefit Analysis

CFP   Common Fisheries Policy

CEU   Civitas EU Facts, available from:
http://www.civitas.org.uk/eufacts/index.php

ECJ   European Court of Justice, based in Luxembourg

EEA   European Economic Area

EU   European Union

EU-27   The 27-member EU

EU-26   EU-27 minus the UK

Eurozone or Euro-area
     The 17-member group of countries using the euro

EFTA   European Free Trade Association

FTA   Free Trade Agreement

GDP   Gross Domestic Product

NAFTA   North American Free Trade Agreement

NGO   Non-Governmental Organisation

WTO   World Trade Organisation

Wrong Horse
     Backing the Wrong Horse, by Ian Milne,
available at www.civitas.org.uk/wronghorse.pdf

Foreword

Britain used to call herself the mother of democracies, but whilst we continue to preach the benefit of democracy to other countries we are increasingly denying it to ourselves. Our armed forces fought in Iraq and are fighting in Afghanistan and Libya to give self-determination to those countries. Meanwhile, back at home, hardly a week goes by when we are not giving further powers to unelected authorities in Brussels or to the European Court of Human Rights, the latter presided over by some 39 judges only two or three of whom have grown up with British traditions of liberty behind them, while the majority know nothing of the concepts of Magna Carta and Habeas Corpus.

Britain is now virtually no more than a province in the Republic of Europe. It is nearly impossible to change, rectify or to sensibly modify any of the stream of regulations that are constantly put upon us. The economic cost is hugely damaging to our competitiveness.

The American War of Independence was fought on the slogan *No Taxation Without Representation*. We now have the modern equivalent: *Regulation Without Rectification*. If one cannot change regulations through elected representatives then democracy is in denial. If you cannot sack those who rule you, you no longer have sovereignty.

This is the Britain we know today. We must reverse it. Like other countries, we could manage perfectly well outside Europe: we are a global trading nation. Britain must discover that democracy means self-governance and that self-governance only works with national independence.

In every respect we would be better off out.

Lord Vinson of Roddam Dene LVO DL
Chairman, Joint House of Lords and House of Commons Better Off Out Committee

1

The Economics of EU Membership

Summary and Conclusion

- Evidence is accumulating that membership of the EU imposes a heavy ongoing net cost on the UK economy—possibly in excess of ten per cent of GDP, over £140 billion a year at 2009 prices. *BN65*

- Long before the 2010 euro crisis, a consensus existed (amongst member-state governments, the Commission itself, NGOs, business and academia) that in the decades to come Continental EU's prospects, as a market and an economy, are dire. That consensus is strengthening.

- As much as 60 per cent of UK exports already go outside the EU, using the author's estimates for the effect of distortions on trade statistics. Since 2000 they have been growing almost 40 per cent faster than exports *to* the EU. Growth in export markets is almost certainly going to occur in the 95 per cent of global population **outside** EU-26, rather than in the five per cent **inside** EU-26. *BNs 58/64/68, CEU*

- That being so, the UK's first priority ought to be to decide how its trading arrangements with the world **outside** the EU should be configured. That decision would condition the extent to which the UK's relationship with the EU Single Market should be changed. Full withdrawal would be one of the options.

The Context: Demography

- The UK accounts for less than one per cent of global population today; the remainder of the EU ('EU-26') represents six per cent of global population today. *BN 58*

- But, by 2050, 39 years from now, EU-26's overall population will have shrunk in absolute terms and aged severely, accounting for less than five per cent of global population. In 2050, more than 95 per cent of global population will be outside EU-26. *BN 58*

- By 2050, EU-26 will have lost 57 million of working-age (15-64) population, more than the entire present-day 54 million working-age population of Germany. In contrast, by 2050, the US will have gained 36 million of working-age population. *BN 69*

1

- Between now and 2050, the 'swing' of working-age population between EU-26 and the USA will be over 90 million. Putting it another way, by 2050, in terms of working-age population, EU-26 'loses the whole of Germany' while the USA 'gains two-thirds of Germany'.

BN 69

- By 2050, the UK's overall population will still represent less than one per cent of global population. UK working-age population will grow by seven per cent; EU-26's will shrink by 19 per cent.

BNs 58/69

GDP and International Trade

- EU-26 appears to be a shrinking market in irreversible long-term structural decline.

- By 2050, EU-26's shares of global GDP and global trade will both have halved, to around 10 per cent.

ACTF

- By 2050 the USA (and NAFTA) shares of global GDP and trade will be as great (over 20 per cent) or even greater than today. China's and India's shares should be similar to those of the USA.

ACTF

- Today, over 90 per cent of the UK economy is *not* involved in exporting to EU-26.

BN 67

- Today, of the UK's exports worldwide (of goods, services, investment income and transfers) around 60 per cent go **outside** EU-26, 40 per cent *to* EU-26 (after adjusting the official figures for the Rotterdam-Antwerp Effect and the separate Netherlands Distortion). Other estimates of the distortion published at:
  http://www.civitas.org.uk/eufacts/index.php result in a split of 53 per cent (Rest of the World) to 47 per cent (EU-26).

BN 64, CEU

- The structure and pattern of UK exports are quite different from those of other EU countries, particularly Germany and France. Only 40 per cent of UK exports are of goods (versus 71 per cent for Germany, 58 per cent for France); 28 per cent of UK exports are of services (versus 14 per cent for Germany, 18 per cent for France); and 31 per cent of UK exports consists of investment income (versus 15 per cent for Germany, 24 per cent for France). Geographically, 63 per cent of German exports and 64 per cent of French exports go to 'EU-26' compared to only 47 per cent for the UK. (*2009 data, not adjusted for the two distortions above.*)

BN66

- A country doesn't need to be **in** the EU to sell **to** the EU. The USA, for example, not in the EU, sells more to the EU than the UK does, without paying a cent to Brussels or imposing an ounce of EU regulation on the US economy. The EFTA countries, not in the EU, export a higher proportion of their worldwide exports to the EU than does the UK.

  BN 62

- The UK has a huge structural deficit on its trade with EU-26.

  BN60

- The EU economic model, of a Single Market grafted on to a Customs Union, is emulated nowhere else in the developed world (and hardly at all in the developing world).

  Wrong Horse

UK Membership of the EU: Net Cost or Benefit?

- Even before the UK joined the Common Market in 1973, cost-benefit analyses (CBAs) predicted negative economic consequences.

  ACTF

- In the last ten years, no respectable CBA has actually concluded that the UK derives a net economic benefit from EU membership. British governments (unlike the Swiss Government) refuse to carry out CBAs of EU membership, almost certainly because they know what the result would be.

  ACTF

- At best, CBAs conclude that the net economic benefit is marginal.

- More recent CBAs conclude that the net economic costs of EU membership are significant, ranging upwards from an absolute rock-bottom minimum annual ongoing net cost of around four per cent of GDP (Milne/Minford).

  BN 65

- A higher net cost of EU membership, seven per cent of GDP or more, may be inferred from Gordon Brown's October 2005 pamphlet (not a CBA as such) published by HM Treasury.

  BN 65

- Minford suggests that EU policies are as pernicious for UK manufacturing and trade as the CAP is for UK agriculture.

  BN 65

- There are well-founded fears that EU policies will soon inflict serious damage on the UK's hitherto highly-successful services sector, especially the City.

2

Eight Reasons Why the UK Doesn't Need the EU Single Market

The EC Customs Union dates from 1957. The Single European Act came into effect in 1992 and superimposed on the Customs Union a costly, tightly-regulated, supposedly harmonised internal market: the Single Market. The outsourcing to Brussels of the regulation of all the City's financial markets, the Social Chapter, the Working Time Directive, Health and Safety and Tax Harmonisation: all are part of the pursuit of the Single Market.

Membership of the Single Market is often said to be vital for British trade. The facts suggest that that proposition is wrong.

FIRST: Customs Unions are redundant

Over 90 per cent of British imports are tariff-free, and those tariffs that remain are very low. Tariffs are only charged on trade in goods; they are not charged at all on trade in services or income. UK trade in goods is well under half of total UK trade, the rest being in tariff-free services and income. The cost of collecting those low tariffs on goods is greater than the amount of tariff actually collected. In other words, Customs Unions are redundant: they have lost their *raison d'être*. That is why, outside the EU, there are simply no significant customs unions at all, anywhere in the world.

BN 70 and Wrong Horse

SECOND: Single Market membership is hugely costly

If, as many assert, the UK is in the EU to get 'access' to the Single Market, it follows that the hidden costs of exporting to the EU—in effect, a tax paid by British taxpayers on UK exports—are absolutely colossal.

Recent studies indicate that a net annual cost of EU membership of ten per cent of GDP, equivalent to £139 billion in 2009, is perfectly plausible. In that year, the sterling value of UK goods exports to the EU was £124 billion. The ratio 139 to 124 is 1.1 times. This means that for every ten pounds of UK goods exported to the EU, British taxpayers paid in addition, for the privilege of 'access' to the Single Market, a hidden tariff—an export tax—of eleven pounds.

BN 65

THIRD: *The haemorrhage of skilled UK jobs to the Continent resulting from the trade deficit*

The UK has a massive structural trade deficit with the EU. In the five years 2005 to 2009, 88 per cent of the UK's alarming trade deficit with the whole world has been accounted for by the EU. Over those five years the accumulated UK deficit with the EU was £135 bn. The UK trades with the rest of the world more or less in balance. It is possible that membership of the Single Market has a detrimental effect on the UK deficit with EU countries.

BN 60

The consequence of this massive deficit with the EU is the haemorrhage of British jobs to the Continent: huge numbers of skilled British jobs being in effect transferred over the Channel (in other words lost in the UK and gained on the Continent). The result of this deficit is an extra two million[1] or so jobs, many of them highly-skilled, in Germany, France and other EU countries, that might have remained in the UK were it not for the UK deficit with the EU. In the context of the UK's own 30 million workforce and high unemployment rate, two million 'lost' jobs is a huge number.

FOURTH: *Over 90 per cent of the British economy is NOT involved in exports to the EU.*

Putting it another way: exports to the EU account for less than ten per cent of British economic output. Within the approximately 90 per cent *not* involved in exports to the EU, 80 per cent is British internal trade (generated by British residents trading with each other), ten per cent is exporting to the world beyond the EU. Yet that 90 per cent still has to impose on its activities the whole of the hugely costly Single Market legislation and regulation.

BN 67

FIFTH: *British Export Growth: better outside the EU.*

British exports to the world *outside* the EU are growing far faster than British exports *to* the EU — 37 per cent faster since the turn of the century.

The main reason why British export growth is almost 40 per cent higher outside the EU is that most EU markets are anaemic, while many markets outside the EU are expanding rapidly. Excessive Single Market regulation may not explain all of EU economic anaemia, but, according to the *Conseil d'Analyse Economique* which reports to

---

1   Lea, R., Global Vision Perspective, *UK-EU Trade creates far fewer jobs in the UK than in the rest of the EU*, 21 April 2008; www.global-vision.net

the French Prime Minister, it is a major factor in the EU's economic under-performance compared with the rest of the world.

BN 43* and BN 68

SIXTH: *British Import Growth: more from outside the EU.*

But maybe, for the British, Single Market membership makes it easier to import goods and services? Not so: British imports from the world beyond the EU are increasing significantly faster (18 per cent faster over the ten years 1999-2009) than British imports from the EU.

BN 68

So, whether British exports or British imports are concerned, the Single Market fails the acid test: overall, there is simply no objective evidence that the UK benefits from being part of it.

SEVENTH: *The proportion of British exports going to the EU, already under half, is declining.*

At present, roughly 40 per cent of UK exports go the EU. Even using more conservative estimates of trade distortions, that figure is still below 50 per cent. And because of the faster rate of growth of UK exports *outside* the EU, by, say, 2020, the split of UK worldwide exports will be something like two-thirds *outside* the EU, one third *to* the EU, rendering the justification of belonging to the Single Market even more tenuous.

BNs 64 and 68, CEU

EIGHTH: *A country doesn't have to belong to the Single Market to export to the Single Market.*

The USA and China, not EU members, with zero votes in the EU Council of Ministers, zero MEPs, zero Commissioners, zero judges at the European Court of Justice, zero civil servants working in EU institutions, having to export to the EU over the EU tariff barrier, each sell more goods to the EU than the UK does, without paying a cent to Brussels or imposing one iota of EU regulation on their domestic economies.

Closer to home, Norway and Switzerland, not EU members, export far more to the EU in relation to their GDPs or populations than the UK—Norway about fives times more goods per capita than the UK, Switzerland about three times more goods per capita than the UK.

BN 62

Those eight stark economic facts constitute a powerful argument for the UK to leave the EU altogether.

3

Sectoral Questions

How important to the UK could a single market in services be, and what could be the benefits/costs?

Most if not all EU 'policies' have promised significant benefits. In practice, such benefits are almost never realised. That is true for the UK; it is also true of other member states. (Disillusion with EU 'policies' is not confined to the UK.)

In financial services, a constant and explicit aim of French and German policy is to boost the role of Paris and Frankfurt at the expense of the City of London. 'Liberalising' this sector across the EU will almost inevitably result in a hugely increased role for the Commission; a steep increase, via Brussels, in the influence of France and Germany compared with that of the UK; and, worst of all, the transfer of even more power into the hands of the judicially-active ECJ, on which British influence is minimal. If British governments, and the City itself, are serious about defending the City's pre-eminent role in world and European markets they will eschew not just further EU involvement but *any* EU involvement.

What is the potential value of a single EU market in energy?

In theory, a single EU energy market could bring benefits for UK consumers, in terms of price, choice and security of supply. In practice, the EU track record in other areas strongly suggests that those benefits will be elusive. Ultimately, an EU 'energy policy' must mean a centralised 'one-size-fits-all' energy policy: otherwise, why bother?

Why would a one-size-fits-all energy policy suit the UK? Member states are very different, energy-wise. Only one electricity cable exists between the UK and the Continent, and only one gas connector. The UK is still oil- and gas- and coal-rich compared with Germany and France. The UK is around 20 per cent nuclear; France is 80 per cent; Germany 30 per cent. Germany's natural historic geo-strategic hinterland, for a thousand years at least, is eastern Europe and Russia. The UK faces west, France south. France's biggest energy producer and distributor (and the biggest in the world) is Electricité de France (EdF). EdF is still the historic bastion (via the CGT trade union) of the French Communist Party, the only major Communist Party in the western world which has not felt the need to change its name. One reason why union reform is so rarely on the agenda in France is that the Communists can shut the country down via the EdF when they choose.

Continental Europe is already heavily dependent on Russian gas. The Commission argues that taking on the role of negotiating supplies in place of the 27 member states is 'better' than 27 nations negotiating separately. The analogy is with the Commission negotiating on behalf of the 27 at the WTO, where in practice France (as she did in the Uruguay Round and continues to do in the current Doha Round) forces its partners to accept *de minimis* reforms. For the UK, a realistic working assumption is that a single EU energy policy—especially one based on the questionable precepts of 'climate change'—would probably do for the UK energy sector what the CAP has done to farming, the CFP to fishing, and what the Single Currency is doing to large parts of the Eurozone.

Competition Policy: the pros and cons of remaining part of the EU legal framework

Given the Continent's dire prospects, the already-tilted EU playing field and the pronounced extra-EU orientation of UK trade and investment, it is by no means evident that, over the next 30 to 50 years, a legal space (for competition purposes) coterminous with the existing EU-27 is the appropriate one for UK business, or that not being inside it would be particularly damaging. It could be that the arguments for repatriating competition law downwards to the territory of the UK, or upwards to a jurisdiction far wider than the EU (perhaps to a beefed-up WTO?) are just as persuasive.

If the Commission/ Council/ ECJ opened up Continental state monopolies and other protected sectors to genuinely free competition, the net gains for the UK—again in theory—could be useful, though unlikely to be dramatic. Any such liberalisation would require huge, sustained and bruising political effort, and probably take a generation to implement. The comprehensive failure of the Lisbon Process[1] (supposed to transform the EU into the 'most dynamic' continent on the planet by 2010), and the unilateral French withdrawal from the core EU principle of 'freedom of movement of capital' (see box) illustrate the futility of the UK's relying on a 'level EU playing field'.

> *In 2008 the French government set up a 'sovereign wealth fund', now in operation, specifically designed to prevent foreign takeovers of domestic firms.*
>
> *In 2011 the French government refused to accept the decision by the technical Anglo-French Intergovernmental Commission that a number of new Eurostar trains for the London-Germany route should be built by Siemens of Germany rather than Alstom of France.*

---

1 The 'Lisbon Process' pre-dates and has nothing to do with the 'Lisbon Treaty'.

Are there sectors where opting out of the EU customs union/single market would put UK exports at risk?

Even inside the EU, UK exports are frequently at risk. British beef and London taxis are just two examples. Given Continental EU's massive structural surplus on its trade in goods with the UK, all the negotiating cards are in the UK's hands. In any case, outside the EU, the UK would be able to use WTO mechanisms to ensure fair trade with the EU. (Many Canadians believe that, pre-NAFTA, the WTO offered them more protection against unfair US practices than NAFTA membership does.)

4

Alternatives to
Full EU Membership

Outside the EU, a UK which declared unilateral free trade with all comers would in theory realise maximum savings compared with being a full member of the EU. The 'Norwegian Option' (used also by Iceland and Liechtenstein) and the 'Swiss Option', which allow European non-EU countries to keep clear of main EU 'policies' such as the CAP and EMU while being semi-detached members of the EU Single Market, involve significant ongoing costs, though less than those that go with full EU membership.

A clean break with the EU under the World Trade Organisation umbrella

- Global multilateral free trade, the objective of the WTO, remains an aspiration. The last thirty years have seen an explosion in the number of bilateral and multilateral FTAs outside the developed world's only customs union, the EU. The EU itself (and, indirectly, the UK, if her EU membership continues) will soon have FTAs with eighty per cent of all the non-EU states in the world. Outside the EU, the UK could choose to join the FTA 'party' as a direct player.

BN 61

- An FTA is partly a contradiction in terms. An FTA may allow the parties free trade with each other, but it implies a measure of discrimination against countries outside the FTA. A radical option for the UK would be, under the WTO umbrella, to eschew FTAs altogether, and unilaterally declare genuine free trade with the whole world (including the remaining EU) buying all its imports at world prices and selling its exports where it could.

- On the face of it, following withdrawal from the EU, a UK which declared unilateral free trade with all comers would realise maximum savings compared with being a full member of the EU. Adopting the semi-detached option *à la* Norway or Switzerland inevitably means being stuck with some of the ongoing costs associated with Single Market membership.

- Following full UK withdrawal from the EU, the UK ought to consider making the Commonwealth the main focus and vector of its global trade policy. In 2050, viewed from the UK, the rest of the Commonwealth will constitute a market nine times greater than that of Continental EU. By a fortunate accident of history, the

Commonwealth will be where much of global GDP and trade growth will occur over the next half-century.

BN 58

- Another possibility, often floated, is for the UK to join the USA, Canada and Mexico in NAFTA.

- Another is for the UK to enter into bilateral FTAs worldwide on a case-by-case basis.

- Yet another is for the UK to join a Global Free Trade Alliance (GFTA), an idea being developed by the Heritage Foundation. The GFTA would not be a treaty; each member would enact national legislation to allow free trade with its partners. It would not be restricted to a specific region, but include countries which voluntarily committed themselves to genuine reciprocal free trade: no tariffs, no quotas, minimum regulation.

Wrong Horse

Sector-Specific FTAs: the 'Swiss Option'

- Switzerland, surrounded on all sides by EU countries, is a member of EFTA, but remains outside both the EEA and the EU. It has had a Free Trade Agreement (FTA) in industrial goods with the EU since 1972.

BN 36*

- Following referenda in 2002, 2005 and 2010 in which the Swiss electorate gave its consent, there are now 120 sector-specific bilateral Swiss-EU accords, each providing for free trade between the parties.

www.swiss.info.ch.eng/politics

- Switzerland retains full sovereign control over the areas covered in the Swiss-EU FTAs. Decisions in joint committees overseeing the FTAs are taken by unanimity: each side retains its veto. The FTAs can be cancelled at any time, and on the Swiss side none requires the transfer of legislative authority to a supranational body.

- With one partial exception, in civil aviation, none of the bilateral FTAs obliges Switzerland to adopt the relevant part of the *acquis communautaire.*

- The main Swiss-EU FTAs cover trade in goods; free movement of labour; technical barriers to trade; reciprocal opening of trade in agricultural products; public procurement contracts; cooperation in matters of justice, police, asylum and migration; taxation and savings; and intra-EU road and rail traffic on Swiss territory. Switzerland (again, following a referendum) joined the Schengen Agreement, providing for free movement of peoples, in 2008.

EEA Membership: the 'Norwegian Option'

- Switzerland, Norway, Iceland and Liechtenstein are members of EFTA, the 50-year-old European Free Trade Association of which the UK was a founder-member.

BN 36*

- EFTA (unlike the EU) is *not* a customs union. Each of its members conducts its own trade policies and sits and votes at the WTO in its own right. None has transferred any legislative competence to EFTA or EEA institutions.

- In 2010 EFTA's secretariat had 90 employees and an annual budget of £15 million.

www.efta.int

- Three of the four EFTA states, Norway, Iceland and Liechtenstein (not Switzerland) are members with EU-27 of the 30-member European Economic Area (EEA).

- The EEA, an international treaty (of which Norway, Iceland and Liechtenstein, the UK and the other 26 EU countries are signatories, as well as the EU itself) came into force in 1994. It provides for an Internal Market between participants: essentially the 'four freedoms' plus provisions in areas such as health and safety, labour law and consumer protection.

www.efta.int

- The three non-EU members of the EEA are unable constitutionally to accept direct decisions by the (EU) Commission and the ECJ, but participate in the decision-shaping of new EEA-related legislation, and, post-enactment, in its enforcement, through joint bodies with the EU.

- The three non-EU members of the EEA make a financial contribution to EEA and EU programmes. In 2009 this was **seven times smaller**, per capita, than the UK gross contribution to 'Brussels'.

www.efta.int

- The three non-EU members of the EEA remain outside:
  - the Common Agricultural Policy
  - the Common Fisheries Policy
  - EU foreign and defence policies
  - EU justice and home affairs policies
  - EU monetary union
  - and any other 'policy' not specifically provided for in the EEA treaty

- With the (temporary) exception of Iceland, the three non-EU members of the EEA have far higher GDPs per capita than all EU members except Luxembourg.

BN 59

- Under the EEA treaty, no contracting party can be expelled from the EEA. After EU withdrawal, whether or not the UK decided to rejoin EFTA, the 'default' position would appear to be that the UK stayed in the EEA and continued to have free trade with its other 29 EU and EFTA partners. (Note that in the other direction, Austria, Sweden and Finland remained as EEA members when they left EFTA to join the EU in 1995.)

5

How the UK Would Prosper After Withdrawal from the EU

The EU: a failed experiment emulated nowhere else

It is often forgotten that the European experiment in post-democratic governance remains just that: an experiment (and a failing one at that). In no other continent has it been emulated. The preferred option of the majority of countries and peoples of the world is the self-governing nation state. In contrast, a small minority of countries, all European, have opted to renounce national sovereignty.

United Nations membership has grown from 51 countries in 1946 to 192 today. Of those 192, no fewer than 165, or 86 per cent, have chosen to function as sovereign nations, whether liberal democracies such as the USA, Japan, India and Brazil, or autocracies such as China and Russia. The remaining 27 countries—fewer than one in seven—accounting for five per cent of global population, are progressively ceding sovereignty to a supranational institution, the European Union.

The EU is in long-term structural demographic and economic decline. It also costs a fortune to belong to. UK withdrawal would result in the British people rejoining the 95 per cent of the world's population who live in self-governing states and successfully trade with each other—and with the EU—multilaterally.

The World Trade Organisation

The UK is a founder-member of the Geneva-based World Trade Organisation (WTO), the world's principal forum for negotiating and supervising international trade agreements. The WTO, like the UN and NATO, is a multilateral, not a supranational body. On withdrawal from the EU, the UK would resume its own seat and vote (which it surrendered to the EU in 1973 on joining the 'Common Market') at the WTO. The UK would then be free to strike up trade agreements with fast-growing countries and export markets such as the USA, Singapore and Australia.

BN 5*

British influence at the WTO is sometimes claimed to be stronger as part of the EU Single Market than it would be if the UK spoke and negotiated for itself in WTO councils. That claim has validity only in so far as British commercial and geo-strategical interests coincide with all or a majority of its EU partners—all 26 of them. When British interests do not so coincide—for example in the regulation of the City, or in agriculture and fishing—it follows that British influence is weaker than it would be if the UK were outside the EU and able to make its own decisions at the WTO.

Since the structure and pattern of UK global trade is quite different from that of its EU partners, there is no *a priori* reason to suppose that, on balance, British interests and those of its EU partners coincide more often than they diverge.

BN 66

It should be noted that in the UN, the World Bank, the IMF and NATO, the other main multilateral institutions set up after the Second World War by the UK and its wartime allies, the UK shows no inclination to surrender its votes or seats or vetoes to mere functionaries of a regional bloc in irreversible long-term decline.

No interruption to EU-UK trade following UK withdrawal

On withdrawal, the EU would continue to trade with the UK. EU-26's biggest single customer worldwide is the UK, and EU-26 sells far more to the UK than it imports from the UK. Under Articles 3, 8 and 50 of the Lisbon Treaty, the EU is constitutionally obliged to negotiate 'free and fair trade' with non-EU countries—which it does. Besides, discriminating against exports would be illegal under the rules of the World Trade Organisation.

BNs 60 and 61

No loss of 'influence' with the EU Single Market following UK withdrawal

After almost four decades of adopting successive treaties, UK influence in EU deliberations has shrunk to a negligible eight per cent. That is the UK vote in the key EU decision-making body, the Council of Ministers, in which member-states have given up almost all veto powers. In practice, eight per cent and zero per cent are about the same: zero.

BN 72

On withdrawal the UK would regain control of key industries such as the City and resume negotiating on its own behalf with trading partners in the rest of the world—including the EU itself. The US and China have zero votes in the Council of Ministers but still manage to out-export the UK to the EU; Norway and Switzerland, not EU members, with zero votes in the Council of Ministers, export far more to the EU in proportion to the size of their economies than the UK, showing that outside the EU the United Kingdom would be perfectly able to continue exporting to the Continent.

BN 62

The UK's trading options after withdrawal

Outside the EU, the USA (by far the UK's biggest single-country export market), the rising Asian superpowers and most of the rest of the world rely on interlocking WTO-compatible networks of free trade agreements. The UK would fit naturally into that system. The UK should also seriously consider transforming the English-speaking London-headquartered Commonwealth into a user-friendly global trade organisation.

BN 58 and Wrong Horse

Other models the UK could consider are the 'Norwegian Option' (used also by Iceland and Liechtenstein) or the 'Swiss Option'. These allow countries to be semi-detached members of the EU Single Market while keeping clear of main EU 'policies' such as the CAP and tax harmonisation; but they still have to impose on their economies much EU legislation and regulation, as well as making annual payments to Brussels.

BN 36*

After withdrawal, the UK would prosper outside the EU

EU membership costs the UK, net, every year, upwards of four per cent of GDP, with no discernible benefit. Some studies put the cost at more than 20 per cent of GDP. On withdrawal, that burden on the British economy would progressively disappear, as EU regulations were removed from the British polity and economy. If, say, ten per cent of GDP were saved every year, the impact after several years, due to the dynamic compounding effect, would be very substantial indeed.

BN 65

6

The Road to Self-Government

The British electorate, in a referendum held on Thursday 19th June 2014, votes to leave the EU. On Monday, 23 June 2014, the Prime Minister and the Leader of the Opposition send the following joint letter to the President of the EU Council, the President of the Commission and the heads of state and government of the other twenty-six EU member states, as well as Turkey (a member of the EU Customs Union), Switzerland (with which the EU has sectoral free trade agreements) and the three European Free Trade Association (EFTA) member states, Norway, Iceland and Lichtenstein, which, with EU-27, form the European Economic Area (EEA):

10 Downing Street
23 June 2014

Dear Herman, José-Manuel, Angela, Nicolas, Silvio etc. etc. …,

UK Resumption of Sovereignty

On 19 June 2014, in a referendum, the British electorate voted decisively to leave the European Union. Her Majesty the Queen, in her capacity as Head of State of the United Kingdom, Australia, Canada and New Zealand, and as Head of the Commonwealth, has graciously consented to her Government's decision to implement the democratically-expressed choice of the British people.

The purpose of this letter is to let you know how the implementation of the electorate's decision by Her Majesty's Government will affect the principal strands of the relationship between the EU and the UK. This letter also constitutes the United Kingdom's official notification of its decision to withdraw from the European Union under Article 50 of the *Treaty on European Union* (as amended by the 'Lisbon Treaty').

Although the British people have now chosen to pursue a different path from that of the other member states of the EU, we wish to emphasise that the centuries-old objective of our policy, of constructive friendship and cooperation with our European neighbours, remains unchanged. A strong, prosperous and peaceful Europe will continue to be a central aim of British policy, and from today onwards we look forward to developing with our European friends and allies a *modus operandi* which will further that objective.

1. Timing

The United Kingdom will become an independent sovereign state and cease to be a member of the EU and its institutions and agencies exactly two years from now, on 23 June 2016, referred to hereinafter as I-Day.

2. EU Law, British Law and Legal Certainty

The UK will cease to be subject to EU law, regulation and case law on I-Day. As from tomorrow, 24 June 2014, only British courts, including the House of Lords and the UK Supreme Court as the highest courts in the United Kingdom, will interpret and apply EU law, without reference to the European Court of Justice (ECJ). Accordingly, from tomorrow, judgements of the ECJ concerning British individuals, corporate bodies and HM Government will not be applied in the UK, but referred to the House of Lords and/or the Supreme Court for determination. EU Directives and Regulations agreed before 24 June 2014 but not yet transposed into British Law will not be so implemented.

Conflicting rulings of the ECJ and British courts arising during the next twenty-four months will be determined by the usual international dispute settlement procedures, including arbitration, for resolving legal inconsistencies between jurisdictions of independent sovereign states.

From tomorrow until I-Day, and from I-Day onwards, EU Directives and Regulations already transposed into British law will continue to be valid (and enforced solely by British courts without reference to the ECJ) unless and until repealed by the Westminster Parliament or the devolved Parliaments and Assemblies in Edinburgh, Cardiff and Belfast.

---

3. Managing the Transition

A new British ministry, the ***Ministry of EU Transitional Arrangements, META,*** headed by a senior Cabinet minister, will be charged, as from tomorrow, 24 June 2014, with the responsibility for managing and negotiating the transition process. META's second-in-command will be a senior Opposition shadow minister. The creation of META will facilitate negotiations by giving our allies and friends in EU-26, the EEA, EFTA and outside Europe a 'single telephone number' for all matters concerned with British disengagement from the EU.

Other ministries (HM Treasury, the FCO, Business, Agriculture and Fisheries, Defence etc. etc.) will report to META on all transition matters. META will be staffed by senior executives from the British private sector, from business, transport, energy, City, farming, fishing, military and legal circles. The latest project-management techniques will be bought-in from the private sector to ensure that the transition process runs smoothly and completes on time. META may invite other ministries to second civil servants to it on temporary contracts. META will complete the bulk of its work by I-Day, but remain in existence for a further two years, to help resolve any 'left-over issues'. By statute, it will be dissolved exactly four years from today.

4. European Parliament

British MEPs will continue to represent their constituents in the European Parliament until I-Day, but will not participate or vote in any new legislation brought before the parliament in the next twenty-four months. Their salaries and allowances will be progressively reduced over this period to reflect their reduced workload. They will resign their seats on I-Day and thereafter take no further part in the parliament's activities.

5. Council, Commission and other EU institutions and agencies

British officials and employees of the Council, Commission and all other EU institutions and agencies will negotiate the timing and terms of their departure with the relevant EU authorities. British representation at COREPER and in other EU institutions and agencies will be progressively reduced over the next twenty-four months, in co-operation with the relevant EU bodies and the other 26 member states.

6. EU Budget

The UK's monthly gross contributions to and receipts from the EU Budget will be reduced by $1/24^{th}$ on a straight-line basis in each of the 24 months between now and I-Day, to reflect the progressive disengagement of the UK from the EU over that period.

7. Trade

On I-Day, the UK will withdraw from the EU Customs Union and UK trade will cease to be regulated by the EU. At the World Trade Organisation ('WTO') the UK will resume its own seat and vote in its own right. Trade between the UK and EU-26 and between the UK and the rest of the world will be conducted as already provided for in the WTO, UN, NATO, OECD and other multilateral treaties, and relevant declarations of the Commonwealth.

8. Defence

On I-Day the UK will cease to participate in EU defence planning, activities and operations, including its arms-procurement agencies. From I-Day onwards, the deploy-ment of British armed forces in the defence of the European continent will be conducted through NATO.

9. Foreign Policy

On I-Day the UK will withdraw from all direct EU foreign policy involvement. Thereafter, the UK will conduct its own foreign policy, through the United Nations and in cooperation with regional bodies and individual states, including the EU and its 26 member states.

10. Economic and Monetary Union (EMU)

The UK will cease all involvement in EMU, including the European Central Bank, on I-Day.

11. Common Agricultural Policy and Common Fisheries Policy

The UK will cease all involvement in the CAP and the CFP on I-Day.

12. Immigration and Asylum

The UK will cease all involvement in EU immigration and asylum matters and resume full and absolute control of its borders on I-Day.

13. International Aid

The UK will cease all involvement in EU aid programmes worldwide on I-Day. From I-Day onwards, UK government aid will be provided directly to recipient countries or through multilateral agencies such as the UN.

14. Other Policy Areas

In addition to the policy areas specified above, the UK, on I-Day, will cease involvement in all other EU policy areas (banking supervision, health and safety, policing, education, regulation of working-time, climate change, human rights, etc. etc.).

15. Enabling Legislation in the UK

A Bill to give effect to the measures set out above will be laid before the House of Commons next week.

-------XXX-------

Her Majesty's Government looks forward to working with the institutions and agencies of the EU and its 26 member states to ensure that transition takes place with minimal disruption.

A copy of this letter is being sent to the Heads of Government (and where appropriate the Heads of State) of the UK's Commonwealth partners; to the President of the United States; to the Heads of State and Government of other countries; and to the Secretaries-General of the United Nations, the North Atlantic Treaty Organisation, the World Trade Organisation, the International Monetary Fund, the World Bank (etc etc). A copy of this letter is also being released to the media and posted on META's web-site, www.withdrawal.gov.uk.

Yours sincerely,

The Prime Minister   The Leader of Her Majesty's Opposition

London, 23 June 2014

Appendix

Global Britain Briefing Note No 58

5 March 2010

The Commonwealth and
British Export Growth 2010 – 2050

'...an overwhelming proportion of the world's GDP growth between 2003 and 2050—nearly 80 per cent—will occur outside of Europe, the United States and Canada'[1]

Summary and Conclusion

For the last 40 years, preoccupied with 'Europe', British governments have neglected the Commonwealth.[2] In the next 40 years, by an accident of history, the Commonwealth will be where much of global GDP growth (and hence of growth in propensity to import) will occur. The Commonwealth, originating in the nineteenth century and functioning in its present form since 1949, is the user-friendly neglected colossus which could enable UK business to fully capitalise on its strengths, focusing on exporting to, and investing in, the growth markets of the future.

The United Nations has 192 member-countries. The **Commonwealth**, which will account for **38 per cent of global labour force** by 2050, has 55 members. The **European Union**, which will account for **five per cent of global labour force** by 2050, has 27 members.

The UK is a member of all three organisations. It is the founder and headquarters of the Commonwealth, of which the Queen is Head. The common language is English, and the political, educational, financial, legal and accounting principles of most members are based on the British model.

---

1 In *The New Population Bomb*, by Jack Goldstone, George Mason School of Public Policy, in *Foreign Affairs*, January/February 2010; www.foreignaffairs.com. This article also cites a World Bank prediction that *'by 2030 the number of middle-class people in the developing world will be 1.2 billion... larger than the combined total populations of Europe, Japan and the United States'*.

2 'The Commonwealth's structure is based on unwritten traditional procedures, and not on a formal constitution or other code... the Commonwealth is a voluntary association of sovereign independent states, each responsible for its own policies.' Declaration of Commonwealth Principles, Singapore, 22 January 1971. Founded in 1931 (though the concept originated in 1884), headquartered in London, the Commonwealth has 55 members, mainly but not exclusively former British dominions and colonies. www.thecommonwealth.org. See also Global Britain Briefing Note No 38, *The Commonwealth: Neglected Colossus?* www.globalbritain.org > *Briefing Notes*.

This Briefing Note takes growth in labour force, here defined as working-age (15-64) population, to be a proxy[3] for growth in GDP, using the latest projections of working-age population from the United Nations.[4] It concludes that the rest of the Commonwealth will represent a market **over nine times greater** than that of the rest of the EU (*Table 5 below*) by 2050. Similar analyses by firms in Germany, France, the United States and China will have reached similar conclusions: competition to export to and invest in the developing world will be fierce. British exporters will need to maximise their strengths: which is why, over the next 40 years, the Commonwealth has the potential to become a valuable component of British trade policy.

Salient Points from the Tables in the Statistical Appendix below

- In 2010, ninety-nine point one per cent (99.1 per cent) of global population lives outside the UK. By 2050, that percentage will have increased to 99.2 per cent.

  Table 1

- In the 40-year span between 2010 and 2050 the world's labour force will increase by thirty per cent, from 4.5 billion to 5.9 billion.

  Table 2

- Over that period, with one exception, every continent on the planet will experience growth in its labour force. **The exception is Europe.**

  Table 2

- Within EU-27, amongst the five biggest economies, the UK is the exception: its labour force grows between 2010 and 2050, while the labour forces of Germany, France, Italy and Spain all shrink.

  Table 3

- Between 2010 and 2050 the European Union (EU-27) experiences a loss in labour force of 16 per cent or 54 million. In effect, over that period, EU-27 '*loses the whole of Germany*', since Germany's entire labour force is currently 54 million.

  Table 3

---

3 Growth in labour force is not the only driver of growth in consumer demand, and growth in consumer demand is not the only driver of growth in GDP. Nevertheless, the associations are strong in developed economies, less strong in poor and developing countries.

4 Population Division of the Department of Economic and Social Affairs of the United Nations, *World Population Prospects: The 2008 Revision*; http://esa.un.org/unpp. This is the world's most authoritative source of demographic data.

- The **Commonwealth's labour force** will increase by **60 percent or 825 million** between 2010 and 2050.

  Table 4

- From the perspective of British exporters and investors, the labour force of the rest of the Commonwealth (C-54) grows between 2010 and 2050 by 822 million, while the labour force of the rest of the European Union (EU-26) shrinks by 57 million: a 'swing' of 879 million.

  Table 5

- By 2050, 96 per cent of the Commonwealth's labour force will be in Asia and Africa.

  Table 6

- In 2050, the Commonwealth will account for 45 per cent of the Asian and 45 per cent of the African labour force.

  Table 7

- India alone will account for 50 per cent of the Commonwealth labour force in 2050, compared with 57 per cent in 2010.

  Table 8

- The four Commonwealth members of the Indian sub-continent: India, Pakistan, Bangladesh and Sri Lanka, will account for 67 per cent of the Commonwealth's total labour force in 2050, compared with 73 per cent in 2010.

  Table 8

- Outside EU-27, between 2010 and 2050, the **USA's labour force** will grow by 17 per cent or 36 million: **almost as much as the entire 2010 labour force of Italy.**

  Tables 3 and 9

- Over the same period, China's labour force will shrink by 11 per cent, though it will still be three-and-a-half times as big as the USA's in 2050.

  Table 9

- Russia's labour force will shrink by 31 per cent between 2010 and 2050; that of South Korea by 31 per cent; and that of Japan by 37 per cent.

  Table 9

General Conclusions

- The USA will become more powerful than it is today, economically, militarily, politically, culturally.

- Europe, and the European Union as a whole, will decline economically, militarily, politically, culturally.

- **Growth in GDP, market size and equity returns will occur outside Europe.**

- Continental EU will be a shrinking market, relatively unattractive to exporters and investors.

- The tax base of Continental EU will shrink: tax rates and public-sector debt will have to increase.

- Shrinking and ageing population in Continental EU will mean more demand for state-provided healthcare and pensions, with fewer active people to provide them.

- Most EU member-states will see falling demand for houses, schools, factories, shops and capital goods, with falling asset values and investment. This will affect both the tax base and the equity markets on which private pension provision depends.

- Sharply-diverging demographics within the EU will make EU-wide 'one-size-fits-all' policies (monetary, tax, labour market, agricultural, asylum, immigration, environmental etc.) ineffective.

- The political rationale of **integration into a fading regional bloc**—the EU—will become questionable.

- For British exporters and investors, the economic rationale of **integration into a contracting market**—the EU—will become questionable.

Statistical Appendix

Table 1: Total Populations: All Ages					
millions	2010	%	2050	%	Change
UK	62	1[3]	72	1[3]	+ 10
EU-26[1]	436	7	422	5	(14)
China/HK	1362	20	1426	16	+ 64
Commonwealth[2]	2159	31	3239	35	+ 1080
Rest of World	2890	42	3991	44	+ 1101
World	6909	100	9150	100	+ 2241
1 EU-27 minus UK					
2 Commonwealth minus UK					
3 Precisely: 0.9 % in 2010; 0.8 % in 2050					

Table 2: World Labour Force[1] 2010 - 2050			
millions	2010	2050	Change
Asia	2797	3388	+ 591
Africa	582	1311	+ 729
Central and South America	385	463	+ 78
Europe[2]	501	398	(103)
North America	236	274	+ 38
Oceania	23	32	+ 9
World	4524	5866	+ 1342
1 Working-age (15 - 64) population			
2 EU plus Russia and other Europe, of which EU 333 mn in 2010, 280 mn in 2050, reduction 54 mn by 2050			

Table 3: European Union Labour Force[1] 2010 - 2050			
millions	**2010**	**2050**	*Change*
UK	41	44	+ 3
Germany	54	39	(16)
France	41	39	(2)
Italy	39	30	(9)
Spain	31	27	(3)
Other EU	127	101	(26)
Total EU - 27	**333**	**280**	**(54)**
1 Working-age (15 - 64) population			

Table 4: Commonwealth and EU Labour Forces[1] 2010 - 2050			
millions	**2010**	**2050**	**Change**
C - 55[2]	1382	2207	+ 825
EU – 27[3]	333	280	(54)
1 Working-age (15-64) population			
2 The 55 Commonwealth members as at 2010			
3 The 27 EU members as at 2010			

Table 5: British Export Markets: Commonwealth (excl. UK) Versus EU (excl.UK): Labour Forces[1]					
millions	**2010**	**%**	**2050**	**%**	*Change*
C- 54[2]	1341	29.6	2163	36.9	+ 822
EU-26[3]	293	6.5	236	4.0	(57)
Rest of World	2890	63.9	3467	59.1	+ 577
World	4524	100.0	5866	100.0	+ 1342
C- 54/EU - 26	**4.6 times**		**9.2 times**		
1 Working-age (15 - 64) population					
2 The 54 Commonwealth members (excl. the UK) as at 2010					
3 The 26 EU members (excl. the UK) as at 2010					

Table 6: Commonwealth by Continent: Labour Forces[1]			
millions	**2010**	**2050**	*Change*
Commonwealth in Asia	1038	1522	+484
Commonwealth in Africa	256	588	+332
Commonwealth in RoW[2]	88	97	+9
Total C'wealth	**1382**	**2207**	**+825**
1 Working-age (15 - 64) population			
2 RoW = Rest of World			

Table 7: 2050 Labour Forces[1]: Commonwealth as a Proportion of World				
millions	**Asia**	**Africa**	**RoW[2]**	**World**
Commonwealth	1522	588	97	2207
World	3388	1311	1167	5866
Commonwealth/World	*45%*	*45%*	*8%*	*38%*
1 Working-age (15-64) population				
2 RoW = Rest of World				

Table 8: Commonwealth Members' Labour Forces[1]			
millions	**2010**	**2050**	*Change*
India	781	1098	*+317*
Pakistan	110	224	*+114*
Nigeria	86	192	*+106*
Bangladesh	107	149	*+42*
Tanzania	24	70	*+46*
Uganda	17	58	*+42*
Kenya	22	56	*+33*
UK	41	44	*+3*
South Africa	33	38	*+6*
Ghana	14	30	*+15*
Mozambique	12	29	*+17*
Canada	24	26	*+2*
Malaysia	18	26	*+8*
Cameroon	11	24	*+13*
Malawi	8	24	*+16*
Australia	14	17	*+3*
16 most populous (above) in 2050	1322	2105	*+783*
39 least populous (not listed) in 2050	60	102	*+42*
Total: 55 C'wealth members	1382	2207	*+825*
1 Working-age (15 - 64) population			

Table 9: Selected Non-Commonwealth Labour Forces[1]			
millions	2010	2050	Change
China[2]	979	875	(103)
USA	212	248	+36
Indonesia	156	184	+28
Brazil	132	137	+5
Mexico	73	80	+7
Russia	101	70	(31)
Turkey	51	62	+11
Japan	82	52	(30)
South Korea	35	24	(11)
Switzerland	5	5	(0.1)
Norway	3	4	+0.4
1 Working-age (15 - 64) population			
2 China + Hong Kong & Macao			

Source: Population Division of the Department of Economic and Social Affairs of the United Nations, *World Population Prospects: The 2008 Revision;* http://esa.un.org/unpp. This is the world's most authoritative source of demographic data.

Global Britain Briefing Note No 59

13 August 2010

European Union 2009 Prosperity[1] Rankings

Un nuovo 'Sorpasso'?

Italian economy on track to overtake the United Kingdom's?

- In 2009, for the first time, Italy's population reached 60 million. Italy's **GDP per capita** was almost identical to that of the UK, though its GDP (the size of its economy) was slightly smaller (three per cent) than that of the UK.

    Table 2

- In 2009, **German GDP was 54 per cent bigger than the UK's**; French GDP was 22 per cent bigger than the UK's.

    Table 2

- French GDP per capita was 20 per cent higher than that of the UK, and higher than that of Germany.

    Table 1

- In US Dollar[2] GDP terms, the measure used by the World Bank, the economies of all 27 EU countries shrank in 2009 compared with 2008. Overall, EU-27's GDP contracted by ten per cent. Overall, average EU-27 GDP per capita contracted by 11 per cent.

    Table 2 and BN 55[3]

- In 2009, compared with 2008, the economy of China grew by 27 per cent. Japan's grew by three per cent. Switzerland's grew by two-and-a-half per cent. The US economy grew slightly, by under a half of one per cent.

    Tables 2 and 4 and BN 55[4]

- In 2009, the UK remained the eleventh most prosperous country in the EU.

---

1   'Prosperity' and 'wealth' are here defined as GDP per capita.

2   Average sterling, euro and US dollar exchange rates in 2008 and 2009 are given in Table 7 (p. 38).

3   'BN 55' refers to Global Britain Briefing Note No 55, dated 18 September 2009, *European Union 2008 Prosperity Rankings*, at www.globalbritain.org>*Briefing Notes.*

4   'BN 55' refers to Global Britain Briefing Note No 55, dated 18 September 2009, *European Union 2008 Prosperity Rankings*, at www.globalbritain.org>*Briefing Notes.*

Table 1

- EFTA's[5] weighted average GDP per capita was **over double** that of EU-27.

Tables 3 and 4

- EFTA, NAFTA and Japan were all more prosperous than EU-27 in 2009.

Table 4

- In 2009, the GDPs per capita of the USA, Australia and Canada were higher than that of the UK.

Table 5

---

5   EFTA is the European Free Trade Association, comprising Norway, Switzerland, Iceland and Liechtenstein.

Table 1: EU-27: GDP per Capita in 2009		
Rank	Country	GDP per Capita, US $ k
1	Luxembourg	104.0
2	Denmark	56.4.
3	Ireland	50.4
4	Netherlands	48.0
5	Austria	45.8
6	Finland	44.9
7	Sweden	43.7
8	Belgium	43.4
9	France	42.3
10	Germany	40.9
11	**UK**	**35.2**
12	Italy	35.1
	EU-27 Average	**32.9**
13	Spain	31.7
14	Greece	29.2
15	Slovenia	24.0
16	Cyprus	22.7
17	Portugal	21.5
18	Czech R.	18.1
19	Malta	18.0
20	Slovak R.	16.3
21	Estonia	14.6
22	Hungary	12.9
23	Latvia	11.3
24	Poland	11.3
25	Lithuania	11.2
26	Romania	7.5
27	Bulgaria	6.2

Source: Table 2 below

Table 2: EU-27: GDP, Population and GDP per Capita in 2009, ranked by size of GDP			
Country	GDP US $ bn	Population mn	GDP per Capita US $ k
Germany*	3,347	81.9	40.9
France*	2,649	62.6	42.3
UK	*2,175*	*61.8*	*35.2*
Italy*	2,113	60.2	35.1
Spain*	1,460	46.0	31.7
Netherlands*	792	16.5	48.0
Belgium*	469	10.8	43.4
Poland	430	38.2	11.3
Sweden	406	9.3	43.7
Austria*	385	8.4	45.8
Greece*	330	11.3	29.2
Denmark	310	5.5	56.4
Finland*	238	5.3	44.9
Portugal*	228	10.6	21.5
Ireland*	227	4.5	50.4
Czech R	190	10.5	18.1
Romania	161	21.5	7.5
Hungary	129	10.0	12.9
Slovak R*	88	5.4	16.3
Luxembourg*	52	0.5	104.0
Slovenia*	48	2.0	24.0
Bulgaria	47	7.6	6.2
Lithuania	37	3.3	11.2
Latvia	26	2.3	11.3
Cyprus*	25	1.1	22.7
Estonia	19	1.3	14.6
Malta*	7	0.4	18.0
EU-27	**16,388**	**498.8**	**32.9**
of which: Eurozone*	12,458	327.5	38.0
Non-Eurozone	3,930	171.3	22.9

* *the 16-member Eurozone at end-2009*

Table 3: EFTA[6]#: GDP, Population and GDP per Capita in 2009			
	GDP US $ bn	Population mn	GDP per Capita US $ k
Switzerland	500	7.7	64.9
Norway	382	4.8	79.6
Iceland	12	0.3	40.0
EFTA	**894**	**12.8**	**69.8**

 # Data on Liechtenstein, an EFTA member, not available

Table 4: 2009: NAFTA[7], EFTA[8], EU-27 and Japan			
Country	GDP US $ bn	Population mn	GDP per Capita US $ k
USA	14,256	307.0	46.4
Canada	1,336	33.7	39.6
Mexico	875	107.4	8.1
NAFTA	**16,467**	**448.1**	**36.7**
Switzerland	500	7.7	64.9
Norway	382	4.8	79.6
Iceland	12	0.3	40.0
EFTA	**894**	**12.8**	**69.8**
Japan	5,068	127.6	39.7
EU-27	**16,388**	**498.8**	**32.9**

---

6 EFTA is the European Free Trade Association, comprising Norway, Switzerland, Iceland and Liechtenstein.

7 NAFTA is the North American Free Trade Agreement, comprising the USA, Mexico and Canada.

8 EFTA is the European Free Trade Association, comprising Norway, Switzerland, Iceland and Liechtenstein.

Table 5: 2009: Anglo-area 'Five' ranked by GDP per capita				
Rank	Country	GDP US $ bn	Population mn	GDP per Capita US $ k
1	Australia	925	21.9	42.2
2	USA	14,256	307.0	46.4
3	UK	2,175	61.8	35.2
4	Canada	1,336	33.7	39.6
5	New Zealand	125	4.3	29.1
	Anglo-area '5'	18,817	428.7	43.9

Table 6: 2009 GDP per capita: Selected Developing Countries			
Country	GDP US $ bn	Population mn	GDP per Capita US $ k
Brazil	1,572	193.7	8.1
Russia	1,231	141.9	8.7
India	1,296	1155.0	1.1
China (excl. HK)	4,909	1331.0	3.7
Turkey	617	74.8	8.2

Table 7: Average £ exchange rates		
2008: £1 bought:	€ 1.256	$ 1.847
2009: £1 bought:	€ 1.122	$ 1.565
Change 2009 v. 2008	minus 11%	minus 15%
Source: ECB Monthly Bulletin, June 2010, p. S 73, www.ecb.int		

Sources:

1. Source of GDP and Population Data: *World Bank: World Development Indicators Database.* www.worldbank.org/data. Data is for 2009. GDP is nominal. The figures quoted are in US dollars at current (i.e. 2009) prices and exchange rates, *not* adjusted for purchasing power parities (PPPs), which are subjective, being based on the cost of a theoretical 'representative' basket of consumer goods and services in each country.

2. This annual Global Britain publication is the sixth to have been compiled using the same World Bank statistics, the same assumptions and the same methodology. Thus, the data set out in the six most recent *European Union Prosperity Rankings Briefing Notes*, including this one, are comparable and consistent.

Global Britain Briefing Note No 60

29 October 2010

Eighty-eight Per Cent of the UK Trade Deficit Over the Last Five Years Was With EU-26

In 2009 the UK traded in deficit with sixteen of its twenty-six EU partners.
UK exports contracted sharply compared with 2008; so did imports.

The UK Gross Contribution to EU Institutions continued its inexorable upward march, costing the British taxpayer £48 million per day in 2009.

- The UK current account balance ('trade deficit') with the whole world, having reached alarming levels in 2006 and 2007, contracted significantly in 2008 and 2009.

Table 1

- The contraction in 2009 occurred in spite of a large increase in the UK deficit with EU-26. The UK **deficit with the world outside the EU**, strongly negative in 2008, almost disappeared in 2009 (a deficit of £1.1 bn.

Table 2

Table 1: UK Current Account Deficit with World 2005 – 2009*					
Year	2005	2006	2007	2008	2009
£ bn	32.8	44.9	36.5	23.8	15.5

- Cumulatively, over the period 2005—2009, the UK deficit with EU-26 accounted for 88 per cent of the deficit with the whole world. Cumulatively, on **its trade with the world outside the EU**, the UK has been almost in balance

Table 2

Table 2: UK Current Account Balance With EU-26 and Rest Of World*						
Year	2005	2006	2007	2008	2009	Cumul. '05 – '09
Balance UK/EU-26 £ bn	(40.6)	(35.5)	(38.5)	(5.5)	(14.4)	(134.5)
Balance UK/Rest of World £ bn	+7.8	(9.4)	+2.0	(18.3)	(1.1)	(19.0)
Balance UK/Whole World £ bn	(32.8)	(44.9)	(36.5)	(23.8)	(15.5)	(153.5)
UK Deficit with EU-26 as a proportion of UK Deficit with World						*88%*

- The value of UK exports to EU-26 shrank by almost a fifth in 2009 compared to 2008; the shrinkage in UK exports to the Rest of the World was less.

Table 3

Table 3: Shrinkage of UK Exports from 2008 to 2009*			
£ bn	2008	2009	Difference
Exports to EU-26	342	277	(19%)
Exports to Rest of World	359	300	(16%)
Exports to World	*701*	*577*	*(18%)*

- On its trade with the whole world in 2009 the UK ran a large deficit on goods, (£82 bn), offset by surpluses on services and income.

Table 4

Table 4: UK Current Account in 2009: £ bn*					
	Goods	Services	Income	Transfers	Total
Exports:					
To EU-26	124	64	77	12	277
To Rest of World	104	95	97	5	300
Exports to World	228	159	174	17	577
Exports to World as percentage	40	28	30	3	100
Imports:					
From EU-26	161	55	58	17	291
From Rest of World	148	54	85	14	302
Imports from World	309	109	143	31	593
Balances:					
With EU-26	(37)	9	20	(6)	(14)
With Rest of World	(45)	41	11	(9)	(2)
With World	(82)	50	31	(15)	(16)

- In 2009, UK exports of Goods ('visibles') accounted for 40 per cent of all UK exports worldwide. 'Invisibles' (Services, Income and Transfers) accounted for 60 per cent of all UK exports worldwide. In other words, for the UK, **the export value of 'invisibles' is 50 per cent** (60 divided by 40) **higher than the export value of 'visibles'.**

Table 4

- In 2009, the UK increased its surplus (+ £11.5 bn) on its trade with the USA, though it was less than the surpluses of more than £17 bn recorded in 2005, 2006 and 2007. The cumulated trade surplus with the USA over the five–year period 2005-2009 is £75 bn, compared with a cumulative deficit with EU-26 over the same period of £135 bn.

Table 5

Table 5: Balances: Largest Surpluses and Deficits in 2008: £ bn*		
Surpluses	Netherlands	12
	USA	12
	Luxembourg	8
	Switzerland	8
	Australia	6
Deficits	China + Hong Kong	(19)
	Norway	(12)
	Germany	(12)
	EU Institutions	(7)
	France	(6)

- In 2009, the **UK Gross Contribution to EU Institutions** hit a new record of **£17.4 bn**, **equivalent to £48 million per day**. UK Gross and Net Contributions are set to rise sharply from 2009 onwards as a result of the abandonment by Mr Blair, then Prime Minister, on 17 December 2005, of part of the Fontainebleau Abatement.

Table 6

Table 6: UK Contributions to EU Institutions: £ bn*						
	2005	2006	2007	2008	2009	Cum. 05 – 09
Gross Contribution	(15.1)	(15.4)	(15.8)	(16.4)	(17.4)	(80.1)
Receipts from 'Brussels'	9.1	9.3	8.5	9.8	10.7	47.4
Net Contribution	(6.0)	(6.1)	(7.3)	(6.6)	(6.7)	(32.7)

Notes and Data Sources

* *The Pink Book 2010*, 31 July 2010, www.statistics.gov.uk > Economy > Balance of Payments > The Pink Book 2010

a) Payments to and from supra- and international organisations, and remittances by expatriates, which are included in 'Transfers', are not strictly speaking 'Trade', but a large proportion of them are trade-related. HM Government itself justifies UK net payments to the EU on the grounds (unsupported by any evidence) that '*the UK needs to be in the EU for trade*'.

The data above is not adjusted for the Rotterdam-Antwerp Effect (described on pages 200 and 201 of the *Pink Book 2010*) or the separate Netherlands Distortions (see *Global Britain Briefing Note No 52*, 'UK plc's Export Growth is Coming from Outside the EU', 2 November 2008). The effect of these two distortions is to significantly overstate (in the *Pink Book*) the value of UK exports to EU-26.

Global Britain Briefing Note No 61

7 January 2011

The EU *has* to Negotiate Free Trade Agreements with Third-Parties — and It Does

*The Lisbon Treaty obliges the EU to negotiate Free Trade Agreements (FTAs)
with a member-state that wishes to withdraw, as well as with states that are not EU
members. The EU will soon have FTAs with 80 per cent of all non-EU countries.*

A. The European Union's constitutional obligation to negotiate with a member-state wishing to withdraw voluntarily from the Union, and to negotiate Free Trade Agreements with the departing member-state

The EU's constitution is the Treaty of Lisbon[1] signed in Lisbon on 13 December 2007. For the first time in the EU's history, this treaty/constitution spells out member-states' freedom to withdraw from the Union.[2]

The operative treaty clause is **Article 50**, *Treaty on European Union*,[3] which says:

> Any Member-State may decide to withdraw from the Union in accordance with its own constitutional requirements... the Union shall negotiate and conclude an agreement with that State... taking account of the framework for its future relationship with the Union...

The Union's constitutional obligation to negotiate free trade agreements with states that are not members of the Union is spelt out in two other Articles of the *Treaty on European Union:*

Article 3 [5] says: In its relations with the wider world, the Union **shall** contribute to... free and fair trade...

---

1 *The Treaty of Lisbon in Perspective*, ISBN 978-0-9558262-0-7, British Management Data Foundation, February 2008; www.bmdf.co.uk   www.eurotreaties.com

2 A member-state's freedom to withdraw from the Union has always existed and has been re-affirmed by successive British governments, whose position — rightly — is that the Westminster parliament is sovereign.

3 A sub-section of the Treaty of Lisbon.

Article 8 [1] says: The Union **shall** develop a special relationship with neighbouring countries, aiming to establish an area of prosperity and good neighbourliness... characterised by close and peaceful relations based on co-operation. [Emphasis added.]

(Note, in these two extracts, the word **'shall'**. 'Shall' *obliges* the Union to '*contribute to free and fair trade*' and to '*develop a special relationship etc.*'; 'may' would not.)

Article 8 [2] says: For the purposes of [the preceding paragraph] the Union may conclude specific agreements with the countries concerned...

In Article 8 [2], the word 'may' indicates that free trade could exist between the EU and other countries in the absence of '*specific [EU] agreements*', the parties relying (for example) on the provisions of World Trade Organisation treaties.

B. The EU will soon have free trade agreements with 80 per cent of all the non-EU countries in the world

At present[4] the EU has free trade agreements with 63 countries outside the EU. The EU is also negotiating free trade agreements[5] with another 63 non-EU countries. It is considering opening negotiations with a further 12 non-EU countries. If all these negotiations succeed, the EU will have free trade agreements with **138 non-EU countries.**

There are approximately 200 countries/states[66] in the world. Of those 200, twenty-seven are EU members. So the **total number of non-EU member-countries in the world is 173.**

If EU negotiations underway succeed, the EU will have free trade agreements with 138 of the world's 173 non-EU members: **a proportion of 80 per cent.**

---

4 October 2010.

5 http://ec.europa.eu/trade/issues/bilateral/index en.htm

6 The United Nations has 192 member-countries; the World Bank lists 213 independent territories: average 202.

Global Britain Briefing Note No 62

7 January 2011

A Country Doesn't Need to Belong to the EU to Trade with It

*The EU will soon have Free Trade Agreements with 80 per cent
of all the non-EU countries in the world[1]*

Several non-EU countries already export more to the EU than does the UK

A. The USA exports more in absolute terms to the EU than does the UK

The USA is not an EU member. It has zero votes in the EU Council of Ministers and no MEPs in the European Parliament. The USA doesn't pay a cent to 'Brussels' (the UK paid £48 million *per day* to 'Brussels' in 2009) and doesn't have to impose one iota of EU regulation on its domestic economy. The USA has no Free Trade Agreement with the EU, and consequently has to export to the EU over the EU's Common External Tariff (customs duties) and quotas.

Nevertheless, the USA exports more to the EU than the UK. In 2009, US exports to the EU were £407 billion; British exports to the EU were £277 bn.[2]

---

1 See Global Britain Briefing Note No 61, *The EU has to negotiate Free Trade Agreements with Third-Parties – and it does,* 7 Jan 2011, www.globalbritain.org > *Briefing Notes*

2 In calendar 2009 US exports (goods, services, receipts of income and transfers) to EU-27 were $ 637,462 million. Those exports, at the average 2009 exchange rate of £1 = $1.57, were equivalent to £ 407,027 million.

In calendar 2009, US exports (goods, services, receipts of income and transfers) to the UK were $ 154,966 million, equivalent to £98,704 million.

Thus, in calendar 2009, US exports (goods, services, receipts of income and transfers) to EU-26 (EU-27 less the UK) were equivalent to £308,323 (£407,027 less £98,704).

In 2009 UK exports (goods, services, receipts of income and transfers) to EU-26 were £277,014 million.

Thus, in 2009, US exports (goods, services, receipts of income and transfers) to EU-26 (£308,323) were greater than UK exports (goods, services, receipts of income and transfers) to EU-26 (£277,014). And US exports (goods, services, receipts of income and transfers) to the EU as a whole, including the UK (i.e. EU-27), were greater, at £407,027, than UK exports (goods, services, receipts of income and transfers) to EU-26 (£277,014).

B. China exports more goods to the Eurozone[3] than does the UK

China is not an EU member. It has zero votes in the EU Council of Ministers and no MEPs in the European Parliament. China doesn't pay a cent to 'Brussels' (the UK paid £48 million *per day* to 'Brussels' in 2009) and doesn't have to impose one iota of EU regulation on its domestic economy. China has no Free Trade Agreement with the EU, and consequently has to export to the EU over the EU Common External Tariff (customs duties) and EU quotas. Nevertheless, China exports more goods to the EU than the UK (and will soon no doubt be exporting more services to and receiving more income from the EU than the UK).

In the year ended 31 March 2010, Chinese goods exports to the 16-member Eurozone were £141 bn, greater than the value of British exports of goods to the Eurozone of £125 bn.[4]

C. Norway and Switzerland export to the EU far more in proportion to their populations than does the UK

Norway and Switzerland each has a free trade agreement with the EU, Norway through its membership of the European Economic Area (EEA), Switzerland through bilateral (i.e. Swiss-EU) sectoral free-trade agreements.

Norway and Switzerland have never been members of the EU. They do, however, make a very modest financial contribution to various EU programmes. In 2009, together, Norway and Switzerland paid £168 million into such programmes (compared with the £17.43 billion that the UK paid to the EU in 2009). *Per capita* of their respective populations, Norway and Switzerland combined paid £13.70 to the EU in 2009; the UK paid **twenty-one times as much**: £285.30, to the EU in 2009.

Table 1 shows that EFTA members Norway and Switzerland export to the EU, **per capita** of their respective populations, over **five times** (Norway) and **three times** (Switzerland) by value as much goods as the UK.

The table also shows that the percentages of Norwegian and Swiss worldwide goods exports going to the EU are significantly higher than the equivalent UK percentage.

Sources: US Bureau of Economic Analysis: www.bea.gov/international, *and United Kingdom Balance of Payments: The Pink Book 2010:* www.statistics.gov.uk

3   In 2009 the Eurozone accounted for 76% of EU-27 GDP, 66% of EU-27 population and 86% of UK exports to EU-26; that Chinese goods exports [to the Eurozone] exceed British exports of goods to the Eurozone is almost certainly likely to be true of the EU as a whole.

4   Source: Monthly Bulletin, European Central Bank, October 2010, *Geographical Breakdown of Current Account,* www.ecb.int

Table 1: Exports of Goods to the EU by Norway, Switzerland and the UK in 2007			
	Norway	*Switzerland*	*UK*
Goods exports to the EU in 2007, £ bn[a]	55.0	52.8	127.8
Population in 2007, million[b]	4.71	7.55	61.03
Goods exports to the EU per capita in 2007, £	11,677	6,993	2,095
Goods exports to the EU per capita in 2007, indexed on UK = 100	*557*	*334*	*100*
Goods exports to EU/Goods exports worldwide	81%[a]	62%[a]	55%[c]
a: Table 319, Statistical Yearbook of Norway 2009, www.ssb.no/english; *£1= $2.00*			
b: World Bank: World Development Indicators Database. www.worldbank.org/data			
c: Table 9.4, UK Balance of Payments: The Pink Book 2010: www.statistics.gov.uk .			
Data on geographical breakdown of exports of services and receipts of income and transfers, and on goods for 2008 and 2009, not available for Norway. Data not adjusted for the Rotterdam-Antwerp Effect. (See pp. 53-56)			

Global Britain Briefing Note No 63

7 January 2011

The Proper Definition of 'Trade'

The word 'trade' is often used, carelessly and wrongly, to mean 'trade-in-goods only. The proper definition encompasses trade in goods, services, income and transfers.

'**Trade'** between countries consists of exports and imports of goods, services, income and transfers. 'Goods' are sometimes described as 'visibles', while 'services, income and transfers' are sometimes described as 'invisibles'.

'**Goods'** are physical things such as commodities (e.g. oil or iron ore), agricultural produce, machinery, consumer goods and vehicles.

'**Services'** are services such as international transport, travel, financial and business services, engineering and legal and accountancy services, and royalties on intellectual property such as inventions, patents, music or literature.

'**Income'** comprises income flows such as dividends and interest earned by investors in one country on their investments in another country.

'**Transfers'** are financial flows such as payments by a country's government to international or supranational organisations, or remittances by workers in one country to their relatives in another country.

Internationally and nationally, the *Balance of Payments Current Account* is the set of statistics which contains trade data analysed by the main categories listed above, as well as by sub-categories, and geographically (by country-of-destination for exports and by country-of-origin for imports). In the statistical jargon, exports are 'credits' and imports are 'debits'. The differences between credits and debits are 'balances'; these represent countries' 'trade surpluses' and 'trade deficits' with one another.

The Importance of Income

The last 25 years have seen a massive increase in the amount of foreign direct investment (FDI) worldwide. The UK's manufacturing, services and financial services industries are a major factor in global FDI, both as investors overseas and as recipients, usually ranking first or second in the world for both outward and inward transactions. During the same period, the 'City', which accounts for around a fifth of the total GDP of the UK, has increased its share of the world market for financial services, and is currently the premier global financial centre.

The economic impact of FDI and the City is reflected as 'Income' in the Current Account of the Balance of Payments. Table 1 shows that the value of UK earnings classified as 'Income' now outstrips the earnings from exports of 'Services', and is not far behind earnings from exports of 'Goods'.[1]

Table 1: UK Exports Worldwide by Category: 2009					
	Goods	Income	Services	Transfers	Total
Value £ bn	228	174	159	17	577
Percentage	*39%*	*30%*	*28%*	*3%*	*100%*

Source: UK Balance of Payments:The Pink Book 2010, Table 9.1 www.statistics.gov.uk

The specific reasons for including 'Income' in the definition of 'trade' are:

- Earnings on foreign direct investment (FDI), a major component of 'income' (Table 2) are conceptually similar to earnings derived from trade in goods and trade in services. **FDI, exports of goods and exports of services are different ways of supplying foreign markets**—usually complementary: as much as half of all international trade in goods is between fellow-subsidiaries of multinational companies. A pound remitted in the form of dividends or interest (a receipt of income) from, say, a US subsidiary of Rolls-Royce is just as valuable to its British parent company as the proceeds of selling a jet engine to Boeing (an export of goods) or the proceeds of an engine-maintenance contract with an American airline (an export of services).

- At present, the earnings from UK FDI overseas account for around two-fifths (42 per cent to be exact) of all 'income' on current account [Table 2]. **The remaining approximately three-fifths of 'income' on current account reflects, broadly speaking, the activities of the City of London** and other UK financial centres (notably Edinburgh) [Tables 2 and 3]. (Some of that activity is also 'captured' in the services category as well as in the income category. For example, on a UK bank loan to an overseas customer, the associated arrangement fees would be classified as an export of 'services'.) However, the much larger flows of loan interest would be classified as a receipt (i.e. an export) of 'income'. A very small proportion of 'income' [Table 2] consists of 'compensation of employees', for which the trade

---

1 For an analytical comparison of the German, French and British current accounts in 2009, see Global Britain Briefing Note No 66, Exports of Germany, France and the UK in 2009, 7 January 2011.

justification might be argued to be tenuous: but for the sake of consistency with the UK and international current account statistics, it seems appropriate to regard them as 'trade'.

Table 2: Breakdown of Income by Category: 2009		
	£ bn	%
Earnings on Direct Investment Abroad	73	42
Total Earnings on Portfolio Investm. Abroad	55	32
Earnings on other Investment Abroad*	45	26
Compensation of Employees	1	
Total Investment Income	**174**	*100*
of which earnings on banking transactions		

Source: UK Balance of Payments:The Pink Book 2010, Table 4.1 www.statistics.gov.uk

Table 3: Breakdown of Investment Income by Type: 2009: £ bn	
Monetary financial institutions	62
Other [private] sector investors	109
Central govt. and public corps.	2
Total Investment Income	**173**

Source: UK Balance of Payments:The Pink Book 2010, Table 4.2 www.statistics.gov.uk

Including 'transfers' in the definition of 'trade' is, on the face of it, more difficult to justify, since in the case of the UK a large part of it consists of the outwards flow (an 'import') of British residents' taxes to Brussels—the UK gross contribution—and the inwards flow from Brussels (an 'export') of farming and structural subsidies.

However, to the extent that the resulting UK net contribution to Brussels is regarded as an 'entrance fee' or 'annual subscription' to the Single Market—in other words a cost of doing business with the EU—it is fair to classify 'transfers' as 'trade'.[2] Other transfers

---

2   The British 'entrance fee' or 'annual subscription' to Brussels is often justified—quite wrongly —as the cost of exporting to the EU Single Market. So considered, it consists of a massive hidden tariff charged on British exports to EU-26.

In 2009, the UK gross contribution to Brussels was £ 17.43 billion. In the same year, total UK exports (goods, services, receipts of income and transfers) to EU-26 were £227.01 billion. That works out at an average tariff of almost 8%.

If, instead of the gross contribution, the UK net contribution (£ 6.72 bn) is taken as the value of the hidden tariff, the percentage tariff comes down to 3%.

consist of UK payments to bodies such as the UN or NATO and of bilateral aid, for which the trade justification is again tenuous: but in view of their small relative size, and for the sake of consistency with British and international current account statistics, it seems appropriate to regard them as 'trade'.

However, worldwide, developed countries do not charge tariffs on services, income or transfers. Tariffs are only charged on imports of goods. In 2009, EU-26 imported £124.33 bn of goods from the UK. Based on the UK's net contribution in 2009 of £6.72 bn, the implied average hidden tariff charged by the EU on UK exports to EU-26 was 5.4%(6.72 divided by 124.33). That tariff is not borne directly by private British exporting companies but by British taxpayers and the economy as a whole; it is also a quite separate burden from the other costs imposed on the economy as a direct result of EU membership such as EU regulation.

Global Britain Briefing Note No 64

7 January 2011

The Rotterdam-Antwerp Effect and the Netherlands Distortion

After taking account of both these distortions, the 'real' proportion of worldwide UK exports going to EU-26 is likely to be closer to 40 per cent than to 50 per cent.

Why the distortions occur

The official British trade statistics are produced by the Office for National Statistics (ONS), an agency of HM Treasury. They significantly overstate the real level of UK exports to the rest of the EU, because of two separate distortions, the **Rotterdam-Antwerp Effect** and the **Netherlands Distortion**. The Rotterdam-Antwerp Effect concerns trade in goods, and, to a lesser extent, trade-related services; the Netherlands Distortion concerns flows of income (and flows of capital). The existence of both distortions is recognised by the ONS and its fellow-bodies in other countries, and their distortionary effects can be seen in the trade statistics of EU countries such as France and non-EU countries such as Switzerland. The Rotterdam-Antwerp Effect is discussed on page 200 of the ONS's *The Pink Book 2010*.

The **Rotterdam-Antwerp Effect** arises because the ONS and its fellow-bodies overseas, in compiling their geographical registers of exports, record as the destination of the export the country of the first port of discharge of a consignment, even when the consignment is only in transit on its way to a different end-destination country.

Rotterdam in the Netherlands and Antwerp in Belgium, two of the biggest ports in the world, handle substantial quantities of British exports. Some of those exports are consumed in the Netherlands and Belgium; others are shipped onwards to other EU countries by road and rail; still others transferred to cargo vessels going to other continents. Even when recorded as exports to the Netherlands and Belgium, British goods may not even touch Dutch or Belgian soil, simply being transhipped in the ports of Rotterdam and Antwerp to container vessels bound for—say—Singapore.

A separate distortion, the **Netherlands Distortion**, arises because investments of capital and the income generated thereon are often, for tax reasons, channelled through Dutch 'brass-plate' holding companies by investors (corporate or otherwise) domiciled in other countries. Nevertheless, the income is recorded as originating in or destined for the Netherlands. Luxembourg is another jurisdiction favoured by investors for tax reasons where the same distortion arises.

How big are the distortions?

With the exception of the Banque de France, which has quantified the effect of the Netherlands Distortion on French trade data,[1] none of the national statistical bodies appears to have tried to quantify the impact of these distortions. However, Global Britain, based on long familiarity with the Benelux countries, France and Germany, has made estimates from time to time. The latest, using 2009 data, is set out below.

The magnitude of the distortions is illustrated in the table below, which, in 2009, on the basis of the 'official' data, shows each Dutch person apparently consuming almost five times as much by value of British imports as a German or French person, and each Belgian person apparently consuming almost three times as much by value of British imports as a German or French person. The table also shows each Luxemburger apparently consuming around 50 times as much in value of British imports as a German or a French person.

On-the-ground observation suggests that the per-capita propensity of Germans, French, Dutch, Belgians and Luxemburgers to consume British imports is broadly similar. The 'excess' British imports apparently being consumed by the Dutch, Belgians and Luxemburgers (compared with the Germans and French) constitutes the distortion, which, to give an accurate picture of the real level of their imports from the UK, should properly be allocated to other end-destination-countries within and outside the EU.

The Rotterdam-Antwerp Effect and The Netherlands Distortion: their effect on the 'official' trade statistics					
	Germany	France	Netherlands	Belgium	Luxembourg
A: 2009 UK Exports[1] to:	£ 45.64bn	£35.84bn	£45.55 bn	£17.39bn	£14.71bn
B: 2009 populations[2] mn	81.88	62.62	16.53	10.79	0.50
A/B: UK exports, *per capita of receiving country:*	£ 557	£ 572	£ 2756	£ 1612	£ 29420
1: Goods, Services, Income, Transfers. Source: UK Balance of Payments: The Pink Book 2010: *www.statistics.gov.uk* These are the 'official' figures					
2: Source: World Bank: World Development Indicators Database (quoted in Global Britain Briefing Note No 59, *www.globalbritain.org*)					
See also Global Britain Briefing Note No 32: Foreign Direct Investment: The Netherlands Distortion: 11.9.2004, *www.globalbritain.org*					

---

1   *Banque de France, Balance des paiements et position exterieure: Rapport Annuel 2009,* www.banque-france.fr

If the per capita value of underlying 'real' imports of British goods, services and income into the Netherlands, Belgium and Luxembourg is assumed to be the average of the recorded per capita value of British imports into Germany and France—that is to say, £565—then the adjusted total value of underlying 'real' British imports into the Netherlands, Belgium and Luxembourg would be as follows:

UK Exports: 'Real' versus 'Officially recorded' in 2009			
£ bn	Real*	Recorded	Excess
To Netherlands	9.34	45.55	36.21
To Belgium	6.10	17.39	11.29
To Luxembourg	0.28	14.71	14.43
Total	*15.72*	*77.65*	*61.93*
assuming per capita imports of £ 565 in each country			

It is assumed that half of the total 'excess'—of £61.93 bn—goes to other EU countries, and half to countries outside the EU. To calculate the 'real' proportion of UK exports going to EU-26 in 2009, £31 bn (£61.93 divided by two then rounded up) has to be subtracted from the official total figure of UK exports to EU-26 of £277 bn, to give £246 bn.

The value of UK exports worldwide—£577 bn—does not change. The 'real' proportion of UK exports going to EU-26 is therefore 42.6 per cent (246 divided by 577), compared with the 'official' proportion of 48.0 per cent.

Conclusion

The effect of these distortions is to reduce—in 2009—the proportion of worldwide UK exports going to EU-26 by an estimated 11.25 per cent, from the recorded 'official' unadjusted percentage of 48.0 per cent to the estimated 'real' adjusted percentage of 42.6 per cent.

In assessing the reliability of this estimate the following should be borne in mind:

- The data is for one year only, possibly an atypical year because of the recession which took hold a year earlier. (In 2009, the value of UK exports worldwide was 15 per cent lower than in 2007; UK receipts of income were 41 per cent lower than in 2007.)

- The 'real' level of imports from the UK per capita of the receiving populations in Germany, France, the Netherlands, Belgium and Luxembourg is assumed to be the same as the 'official' average of German and French imports, of £565 per capita.

- It is assumed that half of the 'excess' goes to other EU countries, half to countries outside the EU.

It seems reasonable to conclude that the 'real' proportion of UK exports going to EU-26 is more likely to be close to 40 per cent than to 50 per cent. If 40 per cent is the right percentage, it follows that the proportion of UK exports going *outside* the EU is close to 60 per cent; it follows, arithmetically, **that the value of worldwide UK exports going outside the EU is 50 per cent greater than the value of UK exports going *to* the EU (60 minus 40 = 20 divided by 40).**

Global Britain Briefing Note No 65

7 January 2011

The Economic Cost of EU Membership

*Estimates of the ongoing net cost to the UK of its membership of the
EU range upwards from four per cent of GDP per year*

*In just the 13 years 1997 - 2009 inclusive, the accumulated UK
current account deficit with EU-26 (trade deficit plus the net budgetary
contribution to Brussels) was £218 billion*

In the first decade of the twenty-first century at least eight authoritative cost-benefit analyses (CBAs—listed overleaf) of EU membership have been undertaken in the UK, France, Switzerland and the USA. None has concluded that the benefits—if any exist at all—of EU membership outweigh the costs. Most conclude that the net costs of EU membership are significant, **ranging from a 'rock-bottom' four per cent of GDP to over ten per cent of GDP.**[1]

The results of these eight twenty-first century CBAs should surprise no-one. Well before 1973, when the UK joined the then 'Common Market', economists concluded that the impact of UK accession would be unequivocally negative. Even the government White Papers of 1970 and 1971 predicted negative economic consequences. In October 2005 Gordon Brown, the former Chancellor, published a Treasury paper under his own signature, titled *Global Europe, full employment Europe*. He lists some areas for improvement in EU economies, with estimates of their costs:

EU Protectionism	*7% of GDP*
Competition gap with US	*12% of GDP*
EU Over-regulation	*6% of GDP*
Transatlantic barriers to trade	*3% of GDP*

Those add up to 28 per cent of GDP but do not apply equally to every country. Neither are they wholly attributable to EU membership. Mr Brown did not say whether there might be some degree of overlap in those four categories. His strongest criticisms

---

1   UK GDP in 2009 was £ 1,393 billion. Four per cent of £ 1393 bn is £ 56 billion; ten per cent of 1393 bn is £ 139 billion.

are for protectionism, which he says 'could cost EU consumers up to seven per cent of EU GDP', and regulation. Even if an unusually small proportion of that over-regulation came from the EU and affected the UK, that still puts the annual cost of EU membership at seven per cent at least of GDP, or £98 billion at 2009 prices.

Conclusion

These cost-benefit analyses suggest not only that EU membership imposes annual **net** costs of upwards of four per cent of GDP on the economies of EU member countries, but that **percentages in double figures are perfectly plausible.**

Recent Cost-Benefit Analyses of EU Membership

Complete, Partial and Inadvertent CBAs (Cost-Benefit Analyses) published since 2000

- In April 2004, the New York Fed published *Benefits and Spillovers of Greater Competition in Europe: A Macroeconomic Assessment, Staff Report No 182.*[2] It concluded that '...*increasing competition in the euro area to US levels* **could boost output by 12.4 per cent** *in the euro area as both investment and hours worked rise markedly...*'

- *A Cost Too Far?* by Ian Milne, Civitas, July 2004, put the 'rock-bottom' net cost of EU membership at four **per cent of GDP** rising to 26 per cent due to measures already then in the EU pipeline. This book discusses (pp. 36 - 39) CBAs done by the NIESR, the IoD, the (US) ITC and the IEA between 2000 and 2003. [3]

- In 2005, Minford/Mahambare/Novell published *Should Britain Leave the EU? An economic analysis of a troubled relationship.* Their conclusion: EU membership costs the UK **24.5 per cent of GDP.**[4]

---

2 http://www.ecb.europa.eu/pub/pdf/scpwps/ecbwp341.pdf

3 http://www.civitas.org.uk/pdf/cs37.pdf

4 IEA/Edward Elgar, ISBN 1-84542-3798
http://www.iea.org.uk/record.jsp?type=recommendedBookandID=274 or http://www.e-elgar.com/bookentry_main.lasso?id=3676

- In 2005, the Rt Hon Gordon Brown MP, then Chancellor, published *Global Europe: full-employment Europe*—which, no doubt inadvertently, is a kind of CBA. (See previous page).[5]

- In March 2006 the French *Conseil d'Analyse Economique* (a kind of super-charged Policy Unit attached to the French Prime Minister's Office) published *Politique Economique et Croissance en Europe*. Conclusion: 'Les chiffres confirment bien que l'intégration ne joue plus son rôle de moteur de croissance'.[6]

- In June 2006 the Swiss Federal Government published *Europe 2006 Report*, an economic comparison of Switzerland's joining a) the EU or b) the EEA or c) staying with its current arrangement of sectoral bi-lateral FTAs with the EU. [7] Conclusion: in terms of gross contribution, joining the EU would be **nine times as expensive** for Switzerland as staying with its current arrangements of sectoral free trade agreements with the EU.

- In late 2006 the then EU Commissioner for Entreprise and Industry, Gunter Verheugen, announced that EU regulation *alone* cost € 600 billion a year, equivalent to **5.5 per cent of EU GDP.** In an interview with the *Financial Times*, he said that an earlier figure of €320 billion did not include compliance costs, raising the question of what was covered by that €320 billion.

- In March 2009 Craig and Elliott, in *The Great European Rip-Off,* put the annual cost of EU membership for the UK at £130 billion, equivalent to **9.3 per cent of UK GDP** in that year.

Make-up of Total UK Deficit with EU-26, 1997 - 2009 inclusive

(UK Net Contribution to EU Institutions plus UK Deficit on Trade with EU-26)

- The trade deficit with the EU is not an explicit cost of membership, but is included here to show how much contributions to the EU exacerbate the imbalance. EU anti-dumping policies may contribute to the trade deficit by favouring European producers over UK companies.[8]

---

5   www.hm-treasury.gov.uk

6   http://www.cae.gouv.fr/IMG/pdf/059.pdf

7   http://www.europa.admin.ch/dokumentation/00437/00460/00684/index.html?lang=en

8   Argued by Minford in *Should We Stay or Should We Go?*, IEA/Edward Elgar, ISBN 1-84542-3798, p. 7.

In the 13 years 1997 - 2009 inclusive, the UK paid over £173.6 billion to EU institutions and received back £103.4 billion, resulting in an **aggregate net contribution of £70.1 billion**.

- **In addition**, on its trade (imports and exports of goods, services and income) with the other 26 EU member states, the UK, over the 1997 - 2009 period, recorded an **aggregated deficit of £147.5 billion**.

- The **combined UK deficit** with EU institutions and EU-26 member states over the period 1997 - 2009 was, in aggregate, **£217.7 billion, an average of £16.7 billion per year.**

- The trade deficit reflects the hundreds of thousands (if not millions) of real British jobs effectively exported to the rest of the EU over this period; the contribution to Brussels is a direct burden on UK taxpayers and the British economy.

Make-up of Total UK Deficit with EU-26, 1997-2009 inclusive: £ bn					
	a	b	c = a - b	d	e = c + d
Year	*UK Gross Contr. to EU#*	*UK Receipts from EU#*	**UK Net EU# Contribution**	**UK Deficit on EU-26 Trade**	**UK Deficit with EU-26***
1997	*9.0*	*5.8*	3.2	2.8	**6.0**
1998	*11.2*	*5.6*	5.6	(3.5)	**2.1**
1999	*11.8*	*6.8*	4.9	3.9	**8.9**
2000	*12.2*	*5.9*	6.3	(0.7)	**5.6**
2001	*11.3*	*8.3*	3.0	(4.1)	**(1.1)**
2002	*11.8*	*7.1*	4.7	4.4	**9.1**
2003	*13.0*	*8.0*	5.0	17.1	**22.1**
2004	*13.2*	*8.5*	4.7	25.8	**30.5**
2005	*15.1*	*9.1*	6.0	34.6	**40.6**
2006	*15.4*	*9.3*	6.1	29.4	**35.5**
2007	*15.8*	*8.5*	7.3	31.2	**38.5**
2008	*16.4*	*9.8*	6.6	(1.1)	**5.5**
2009	*17.4*	*10.7*	6.7	7.7	**14.4**
Σ 1997-2009	*173.6*	*103.4*	**70.1**	**147.5**	**217.7**
# abbreviation of 'EU Institutions'					
*total UK deficit with EU-26: UK Net Contribution to EU Institutions plus Trade Deficit					

Source: Table 9.2: *UK Balance of Payments: Pink Book 2010*; for 1997and 1998, *Pink Book 2006*: www.statistics.gov.uk

Global Britain Briefing Note No 66

Exports of Germany, France and the UK in 2009

Analysis by type and by countries-of-destination

The structure of UK exports is markedly different from that of Germany and France

Table 1: 2009: Exports analysed by type: Germany, France and the UK						
All credits on current account excl. transfers	**Germany**[b]	%	**France**[c]	%	**UK**[d]	%
Worldwide exports of each country	£ bn[a]	%	£ bn[a]	%	£bn	%
Goods	731	71	303	58	228	40
Services	148	14	92	18	159	28
Income	149	15	127	24	174	31
Total	**1028**	**100**	**522**	**100**	**561**	**100**
Balance on current account (excl. transfers)	+135		(9)		(1)	
Net transfers to EU Institutions	13		9		7	
a: German and French data converted @ £1 = € 1.122						
b: Source: Bundesbank: Balance of Payments: Statistical Supplement to Monthly Report 3, March 2010, www.bundesbank.de						
c: Banque de France, Balance des paiements et position extérieure: Rapport Annuel: 2009 www.banque-france.fr						
d: Source: UK Balance of Payments: Tables 9.1: The Pink Book 2010: www.statistics.gov.uk						

- In 2009, by value of exports worldwide, Germany ranked first in the EU, the UK second and France third.

- In 2009, Germany traded with the rest of the world in massive surplus (+ £135 bn). Both France and the UK traded with the rest of the world almost in balance.

- The structure of British exports worldwide in 2009 was very different from the structures of German and French exports worldwide. **German and French exports worldwide are heavily oriented to exports of goods, (71 per cent for Germany, 58**

per cent for France). Proportionately, British exports worldwide are more evenly spread between goods (40 per cent), services (28 per cent) and income (31 per cent).

- In value terms, German exports of goods worldwide in 2009 were more than three times greater than British exports of goods worldwide.

- In value terms, **British exports of both services and (receipts of) income were greater than those of Germany or France in 2009.**

Germany and France much more dependent on EU markets than the UK

Table 2: 2009: Geographical Analysis Of Exports[a]: Germany, France, UK									
	Germany[b]			France[c]			UK[d]		
	£ bn[e]		%	£ bn[e]		%	£ bn[e]		%
To EU-26		646	63		334	64		265	47
Of which: to#	F: 94			D: 67			D: 43		
	GB: 89			UK: 46			NL: 43		
	NL: 73			It: 41			F: 36		
	It: 59			NL: 30			It: 17		
To: USA		77	7		40	8		101	18
To: China excl. HK		37	4		11	2		9	2
To: Japan		14	1		8	2		13	2
To: other countries		254	16		129	25		173	31
Total: all countries		**1,028**	100		**522**	100		**561**	100

a: all credits on current account excluding transfers
b: Source: Bundesbank: Balance of Payments: Statistical Supplement to Monthly Report 3, March 2010, www.bundesbank.de
c: Source : Banque de France, Balance des paiements et position extérieure: Rapport Annuel: 2009 : www.banque-france.fr
d: Source: UK Balance of Payments: Tables 9.1: The Pink Book 2010: www.statistics.gov.uk
e: German and French data converted @ £1 = € 1.122
 # F= France, GB = UK, NL= Netherlands, It = Italy, D = Germany
Data above NOT adjusted for the Rotterdam-Antwerp Effect or the Netherlands Distortion

- Whereas under half by value of British worldwide exports go to the EU, almost **two-thirds of German and French exports worldwide go to other EU countries.**

- 53 per cent by value of British exports worldwide went to the world *outside* the EU in 2009, compared with 37 per cent of German exports and 36 per cent of French exports.

- In 2009 British exports were much more weighted towards the US market than German or French exports worldwide. **The US market absorbs 18 per cent of all British exports but only seven per cent of German exports and eight per cent of French exports.**

- German exports worldwide in 2009 were 83 per cent greater in value than British exports worldwide, and 97 per cent greater than French exports worldwide.

- German exports to the EU in 2009 were by value almost double French exports to the EU, and almost two-and-a-half times British exports to the EU.

- German exports to the EU in 2009 were significantly greater by value than French and British exports to the EU combined.

Analysis of UK Exports by Type of Goods and Services

Table 3: UK Exports of Goods by Type in 2009		
	£ bn	**%**
Chemicals	50	22
Intermediate manufactured goods	39	17
Capital goods	29	13
Oil and oil products	25	11
Other semi-manufactured goods	21	9
Other consumer goods	19	8
Food, beverages, tobacco	14	6
Motor cars	12	5
Ships and aircraft	9	4
Other goods	10	4
Total	**228**	**100**

Source: UK Balance of Payments: The Pink Book 2010, Table 2.1, www.statistics.gov.uk

Table 4: UK Exports of Services By Type In 2009		
	£ bn	*%*
Financial	44	*28*
Other business	42	*26*
Transportation	21	*13*
Travel	19	*12*
Insurance	8	*5*
Royalties and licence fees	8	*5*
Computer and information	7	*4*
Communications	4	*3*
Other	6	*4*
Total	**159**	*100*

Source: *UK Balance of Payments: The Pink Book 2010,* Table 3.1, www.statistics.gov.uk

Global Britain Briefing Note No 67

7 January 2011

Less than Ten Per Cent of the British Economy is Involved in Exporting to the EU

Yet EU regulation is imposed on the more than 90 per cent of the economy which is NOT involved in exporting to the EU

In calendar 2008, the proportion of the British economy—defined in the official statistics as 'Final Demand'—involved in exporting goods and services worldwide was just over a fifth, 22.2 per cent to be exact.[1] In the same year, the split of UK worldwide exports of goods and services between the EU and the world outside the EU was precisely 50/50.[2] **The proportion of** 'Final Demand' (i.e. **the British economy) involved in exporting goods and services to the EU was therefore 11.1 per cent** (50 per cent x 22.2 per cent).

It follows that the proportion of UK 'Final Demand' *not* involved in exporting to the EU was 88.9 per cent.

Within that 88.9 per cent, 11.1 per cent was involved in exporting goods and services to the world *outside* the EU. The remaining 77.8 per cent represents the proportion of the British economy concerned with the British domestic (non-exporting) economy.

However, the percentage derived above for the proportion of the UK economy involved in exporting to the EU is overstated. The reason is that two separate distortions in the 'official' statistics overstate the level of UK exports to the EU: **the Rotterdam-Antwerp Effect and the Netherlands Distortion** (see pp. 53-56); and that a third distortion arises **because receipts of income from overseas are not captured in the Blue Book Supply and Use tables** (from which 'Final Demand' is calculated).

The official (Pink Book) data on exports of *goods and services* does *not* take account of the **Rotterdam-Antwerp Effect**, which has the effect of overstating the proportion of British exports of goods and services going to the EU. Consequently, the real, adjusted proportion of the UK economy involved in exporting to the EU is, in the calculation set out above, less than the 11.1 per cent figure derived above from official data.

---

1 UK National Accounts: *The Blue Book 2010*, Table 2.1, Supply and Use Tables for the UK, 2008: www.statistics.gov.uk Data for 2009 not yet available.

2 *UK Balance of Payments: The Pink Book 2010:* Table 9.3, Exports of Goods and Services: www.statistics.gov.uk

Moreover, in the official (Pink Book) data, UK *receipts of income* in 2008 were split 54 per cent from *outside* the EU, 46 per cent *from* the EU. The effect of the **Netherlands Distortion** (pp. 53-56) is to overstate, in the official data, the amount of income originating *in* the EU, and to understate the amount originating *outside* the EU. Quantification of this distortion is difficult, but it is highly likely to be significant.[4] Were it possible to 'aim off' to take account of this distortion, the proportion of UK worldwide income originating *outside* the EU would be *higher* than the 54 per cent suggested by the official data, and, consequently, the 'real' proportion of the UK economy involved in exporting *to* the EU would be even smaller than the 11.1 per cent derived from the official data.

The third distortion arises because *receipts of income* (earned by UK companies from—for example—international banking activities, or as dividends and interest on their investments overseas) **are not 'captured' or separately identified** in the Blue Book Supply and Use[3] tables. Yet, in 2008, the value of those *receipts of income* from overseas was £262 billion. That figure (representing over ten per cent of UK GDP and hundreds of thousands of jobs, mainly but not exclusively in the City) was bigger than the value of worldwide UK goods exports in 2008: £252 billion.

Conclusion

Absolute precision is impossible, *but it seems highly likely that the real percentage of the British economy involved in exporting to the EU is less than ten per cent.*

This conclusion is consistent with the estimate by successive British governments that '*3 million jobs are involved in exports to the EU*',[4] and with the estimate made earlier by Global Britain.[5]

---

3   UK National Accounts: *The Blue Book 2010*, Table 2.1, Supply and Use Tables for the UK, 2008: www.statistics.gov.uk

4   According to Table 1.5 of *The Blue Book 2010*, there were 30.8 million 'economically-active' people in the British economy in 2008. Three million divided by 30.8 million is 9.7%.

5   See *Global Britain Briefing Note No 22*: 90% of the British Economy is NOT involved in Exports to the EU, 20 September 2002; www.globalbritain.org > *Briefing Notes*.

7 January 2011

The Non-existent 'Benefits' of Belonging to the EU Single Market

Over the last ten years, British trade with the world outside *the EU has grown significantly faster than British trade* with *the EU.*

This is true of both exports and imports. So what 'benefit' is the UK deriving from membership of the EU's Single Market?

UK Exports

British exports (goods, services, income and transfers) to the world *outside* the EU are already fifty per cent greater by value than British exports *to* the EU.[1]

British exports to countries *outside* the EU are growing much faster—*almost forty per cent faster*—than British exports *to* the EU. Yet—in theory—there are no trade barriers between member-states of the European Union: zero customs duties, zero quotas, zero non-tariff barriers, zero national protection. In addition, EU markets are geographically close to the UK.

One explanation for the disparity in growth rates of British exports to and outside the EU is the straightforward and easily-observed fact that *EU economies*, and therefore their propensity to import, are *anaemic*, whereas many economies in the wider world outside the EU are expanding rapidly. Not that supplying these faraway fast-expanding non-EU markets is easy: UK exporters often have to export over those importing countries' import barriers: customs duties, quotas and overt and covert protectionism. Once in those markets UK exporters then face fierce local and foreign competition.

In spite of the obstacles to exporting to the world beyond the EU, UK exporters are finding far more growth there than they are in the theoretically trade-barrier-free EU.

The macro-statistical evidence is clear (Table 1): over a relatively long period—ten years—British exports *outside* the EU Single Market are growing far faster than British exports *to* the EU—37 per cent faster.

---

1 *Global Britain Briefing Note No 64*, The Rotterdam-Antwerp Effect and the Netherlands Distortion, 7 January 2011; www.globalbritain.org *> Briefing Notes*.

UK Imports

When it comes to UK imports, a similar pattern can be seen: imports from outside the EU are growing at almost twenty per cent faster than imports *from* the EU (Table 2). This is happening despite the fact that imports from *outside* the EU have to clear the tariff, non-tariff and regulatory hurdles erected by the EU's Single Market. In theory, imports into the UK from *inside* the EU do not face such hurdles.

Although differentials in growth of export markets may begin to explain why UK exports are growing faster outside the EU, it is difficult to see how that explanation can apply to UK imports. The main reason why UK imports are growing faster from outside the EU could simply be that the products and services of non-EU exporters to the UK cost less, once the costs of exporting over the Single Market's trade barriers are taken into account, than imports *from* the EU.

Conclusion

Given that British trade with the world beyond the EU is growing significantly faster than British trade *with* the EU; that the value of British exports to the world beyond the EU is already *50 per cent greater* than the value of British exports *to* the EU; that the UK trades in massive deficit with the EU (and in balance with the world beyond the EU),[2] what 'benefit' is the UK deriving from its membership of the EU Single Market?

Summary

- Over the last ten years, UK exports **(goods, services, income, transfers)** going *outside* EU-26 have grown **37 per cent** faster than UK exports *to* EU-26

- Over the last ten years, UK exports of **goods *outside*** EU-26 have grown **two-and-a-third times** faster than UK exports of goods *to* EU-26

- On the import side, the same phenomenon can be seen: over the last ten years, UK imports **(of goods, services, income and transfers)** from *outside* EU-26 have grown **18 per cent** faster than imports from EU-26

- Over the same period, UK imports of **goods only** from *outside* EU-26 have grown **42 per cent** faster than goods imports *from* EU-26

---

2 *Global Britain Briefing Note No 60,* 88 per cent of the UK Trade Deficit over the last five years was with EU-26, 29 October 2010, www.globalbritain.org *> Briefing Notes.*

Rates of Growth of UK Exports to EU-26 and the world outside the EU (RoW) over the ten-year period 1999 to 2009

Table 1: Rates of growth of UK Exports 1999 to 2009 inclusive			
	Destination	**Average annual % ***	**Index: EU-26=100**
All exports§	To EU-26	4.18	100
	To RoW	5.71	**137**
	To World	4.94	118
of which: Goods	To EU-26	2.05	100
	To RoW	4.78	**233**
	To World	3.19	156
§ of goods, services, (receipts of) income, transfers			
*annual average compound rate of growth 1999-2009, %			
1: Source: UK Balance of Payments: Tables 9.2 and 9.4 The Pink Book 2010: www.statistics.gov.uk			

Rates of Growth of UK Imports from EU-26 and the world outside the EU (RoW) over the ten-year period 1999 to 2009

Table 2: Rates of growth of UK Imports 1999 to 2009 inclusive			
	Origin of Imports	**Average annual % ***	**Index: EU-26=100**
All imports §	From EU-26	4.30	100
	From RoW	5.09	**118**
	From World	4.60	107
of which: Goods	From EU-26	3.95	100
	From RoW	5.62	**142**
	From World	4.71	119
§ of goods, services, (receipts of) income, transfers			
*annual average compound rate of growth 1999-2009, %			
1: Source: UK Balance of Payments: Tables 9.2 and 9.4 The Pink Book 2010: www.statistics.gov.uk			

Global Britain Briefing Note No 69

7 January 2011

The Coming EU Demographic Winter

Between 2010 and 2050, while the USA gains 36 million in working-age population, EU-27 loses 54 million

'The European project, with a black hole forming at its epicentre, will disintegrate'

Allemagne, Chronique d'une mort annoncée, Yves-Marie Laulan[1]

The latest population projections of the United Nations Population Division show that, between 2010 and 2050, **EU-27 will lose 16 per cent, or 54 million, of its current working-age population.** Over the same period, the USA will gain 36 million of its working-age population.

For EU-27, such a drop in its working-age population is the equivalent of the entire present-day working-age population—54 million—of EU-27's most populous country and biggest economy, Germany. The working-age population of Germany itself is projected to drop to 39 million by 2050. (Only five EU-25 countries: the UK, Ireland, Luxembourg, Cyprus and Sweden will see increases in working-age population during this period; Bulgaria and Romania, which joined the EU on 1st January 2007, will experience steep declines.)

To appreciate the magnitude of the contrasting changes in the working-age populations of, respectively, the USA and EU-27, it might be helpful to imagine some divine hand detaching Germany and all its population from the European continent, towing it across the Atlantic and attaching it to the American mainland. The EU, figuratively-speaking, loses the entire productive power of Germany; the USA gains the bulk of it.

Putting it another way: **the 'swing' of working-age population from Europe to the USA in the next 40 years is 90 million**: EU-27 loses 54 million and the USA gains 36 million.

Working-age population (15 to 64 years inclusive in the UN definition) is a proxy for the 'productive' part of the whole population: the men and women whose work and incomes provide for children at one end of the spectrum and for old-age pensioners at the other. Changes in working-age populations may be a better predictor (than changes in whole populations) of countries' economic growth, strength and prospects.

---

1 Yves-Marie Laulan, *Allemagne, Chronique d'une mort annoncée*, Paris: François-Xavier de Guibert, ISBN 2 86839 959 2, 2004.

Table 1: Working-Age (15-64 years) Population in 2010 and 2050: Regions				
Country/region	*2010 mn*	*2050 mn*	*Change mn*	*Change %*
EU-27[1]	**334**	**280**	**(54)**	**(16%)**
USA	*212*	*248*	*+36*	*+17%*
NAFTA[2]	*308*	*354*	*+45*	*+15%*
Anglo-Sphere[3]	*297*	*332*	*+45*	*+15%*

Notes:

1. *EU-27: the present (2010) 27-member EU*
2. *NAFTA: USA + Canada + Mexico*
3. *Anglo-Sphere: USA + Canada + Australia + New Zealand + Ireland + UK*

Source: UN Population Div: World Population Prospects: The 2008 Revision: *Medium Variant*
www.un.org/esa/population

Table 2: Working-Age (15-64) Population in 2010 and 2050: Countries				
Country	*2005 mn*	*2050 mn*	*Change mn*	*Change %*
Germany	54	39	(16)	(30 %)
France	40	38	(2)	(5 %)
UK	41	44	+ 3	+7 %
Italy	39	30	(9)	(23%)

Source: UN Population Div: World Population Prospects: The 2008 Revision: *Medium Variant*
www.un.org/esa/population

See also: *The Demographic Future of Europe—from Challenge to Opportunity*, European Commission, COM(2006)yyy final www.europa.eu.int ; *Eurostat News Release* 48/2005, 8.4.05, www.europa.eu.int; Global Britain Briefing Notes No 26, *Old Europe, Young America*, 25 April 2003 and No 18, *Demographic Change 2000-2050*, 15 February 2002 www.globalbritain.org

Global Britain Briefing Note No 70

7 January 2011

EU Customs Duties

The EU Customs Union is a relic from the 1950s. It is redundant.

The world beyond the EU, where there are no significant customs unions, has moved on.

As part of the EU Customs Union (which also includes a non-EU member, Turkey), the UK does not 'own' the customs duties (also known as 'tariffs') it charges on imports of goods into the UK originating outside the Customs Union. The UK merely collects the customs duties on behalf of the EU and hands them over to Brussels, less a 'handling fee' of 25 per cent of the amounts collected. EU customs duties are a tax on British manufacturers and consumers.

In 2009, the UK charged £2.6 bn in customs duties, retained a quarter of that, £0.65 bn, as the handling fee, and handed nearly £2.0 bn to 'Brussels' as part of the UK Gross Contribution. The £2.6 bn gross collected amounted to one half of one per cent of the total UK 'tax take' of £515 bn in the tax year 2009/10.

Customs duties are only charged on imports of goods from outside the EU; moreover, many categories of goods—for example IT equipment—are exempt from duties. In 2009 the value of all UK imports (of goods, services, income and transfers) from outside the EU Customs Union was £304 bn. Over 90 per cent of that sum was tariff-free[1] (duties are not charged on imports of services, receipts of income or transfers). The value of UK imports of goods from outside the EU Customs Union in 2009 was £148 bn, so the average rate of customs duty charged on those imports of goods was under two per cent (1.76 per cent to be exact: £2.6 bn divided by £148 bn).

A Swedish study published in the 1990s demonstrated that with customs duties so low, the costs of collecting them exceed the value of the amounts collected. An additional indirect regulatory burden falls on the importers, freight forwarders and shippers who have to apply customs duties—even those zero-rated—on the goods being imported.

The fact that EU customs duties are hardly worth collecting means that the EU Customs Union itself is now redundant. There is no point in having a customs union if

---

1 See Customs Duties: hardly worth collecting, *Global Britain Briefing Note No 33*, 17 September 2004, www.globalbritain.org > *Briefing Notes*.

the duties collected are insignificant. The world outside the EU has taken the point: there are simply no significant customs unions anywhere outside the EU.[2]

---

2   See Ian Milne, *Backing the Wrong Horse*, Centre for Policy Studies, December 2004.

Global Britain Briefing Note No 71

7 January 2011

'Keeping the Peace' in Western Europe

*Since 1945, no Western European nation has gone to war with another.
This has nothing to do with the European Union.*

- Between 1945 and the mid-1990s, US, British, French and Soviet forces occupied Germany. The Russians have gone home; but US, British and French forces remain on German soil.

- *Keeping the peace in Western Europe* is a euphemism for preventing a Franco-German conflict. France became a nuclear power **before** the 1963 Franco-German *Treaty of the Elysée* which marked those countries' post-war reconciliation. France had the bomb from 1960 onwards; Germany did not. That fact alone made German military aggression unthinkable.

- From 1945 to 1989 Western Europe's defences were deployed against the overwhelming military threat from the Soviet Union. Russia may yet be a threat in future.

- NATO, founded in 1949 as a mutual defence alliance *'to keep the Russians out, the Germans down and the Americans in'*, included the US, Canada, Turkey and almost all Western European nations. Most Eastern European nations have now joined as well. If anything has 'kept the peace' in Europe during the last 60 years, it is NATO.

- Given the above, in the absence of the European Union, which European nation and NATO member would have attacked another? Not Germany, still, 60 years on, under foreign military occupation. Not France, which in 1945 collectively vowed 'never again' after two disastrous world wars. Not the UK, obviously. Of the smaller countries, would Italy have invaded, say, Austria? Would Holland have invaded Belgium? The very idea of any western European nation attacking another after 1945 is preposterous, European Union or no.

- The implosion, 70 years after its foundation, of an artificially put-together multi-ethnic, multi-lingual, multi-faith federation, Yugoslavia, **did** lead to war in Europe. In 1989 another heterogeneous federation, the 72-year old Soviet Union, collapsed.

Guerrilla wars ensued in several of its former provinces. These suggest that the ongoing attempt to create an artificially put-together political federation, the European Union, carries risks for 'peace in Europe'.

The creation of the American federation in 1789, then as now the most vigorous democracy in the world, was followed 71 years later by a devastating civil war: another demonstration that there is nothing intrinsically peaceful about federations—even those with a single currency, a single language and a single legal system.

Global Britain Briefing Note No 72

19 February 2011

How EU Law is Made[1]

*EU lawmaking is a secretive process which neither the UK
nor any other member-state is able to influence decisively*

- Eighty-four per cent of law in EU member-states originates in Brussels.[2]

- Those laws are proposed **in secret** by the unelected European Commission,[3] which has the monopoly power of proposing new legislation (neither the EU Council nor the European Parliament nor any parliament or other institution of member-states has the power to propose EU legislation).

- Those draft laws are negotiated **in secret** by COREPER,[4] the unelected Committee of Permanent Representatives (i.e ambassadors to the EU) of the member states. The UK delegation is known as UKREP and its representative is one amongst twenty-seven representatives.

---

1 Information as at February 2011; voting strength as given in The Treaty of Lisbon in Perspective, February 2008, British Data Management Foundation, pages lxviii and lxx.

'How EU Laws are Made', by Dr Lee Rotherham, Bruges Group, October 2010, gives much more detail, at www.brugesgroup.com

2 This figure comes from an authoritative study by the German Parliament, commissioned by former German President Roman Herzog and summarised by him in an article in *Welt am Sonntag*, 14 January 2007. Estimates by governments of other countries (including the UK) are somewhat lower, but never less than 50%.

3 **Commission:** Commissioners and staff of the Commission are contractually obliged to act in the interests of the EU, not in the interests of any member-state. So British voting power is **zero.** The Commission is intensively-lobbied by trade associations and NGOs; those favoured by the Commission are often rewarded with Commission subsidies.

4 **COREPER:** The UK representative (UK ambassador to the EU) on COREPER is Kim Darroch KCMG. Informal British voting power: one twenty-seventh or **3.7 %.**

- Those laws are then decided **in secret** (sometimes after consultation with the European Parliament) by the Council of Ministers,[5] where the UK has eight per cent of the vote.

- The resulting laws are then executed by the Commission[6] (in which no EU member-state has any vote) and supported by the European Parliament[7] (in which the UK has 72 MEPs out of a total of 736).

- The Westminster Parliament is irrelevant in this process: it cannot reject or amend — even by one comma — laws handed down from Brussels. (National parliaments in other EU member-states are in the same position.)

- All Westminster can do is to rubber-stamp them — which indeed it does — most of the time without even a debate in either the House of Commons or the House of Lords.

- The Luxembourg-based European Court of Justice,[8] which is legally-superior to all courts in member-states, has the ultimate power of decision over the interpretation and implementation of EU law.

---

5 **Council of Ministers:** UK formal voting power in the Council of Ministers is **8.4%** (29 votes out of a total of 345 votes for all 27 EU members). Post-Lisbon, majority voting is the rule in the Council: there are few occasions on which any member-state can exercise a veto in order to prevent an EU policy being adopted.

As and when new countries join the EU, the voting power of each existing member-state is automatically reduced. One consequence is to give more power to the unelected Commission.

6 **Commission:** See note 3.

7 **European Parliament:** There are 736 MEPs in total of whom 72 — 9.8% — represent British constituencies.

In practice, British voting power is far smaller than 9.8%, since the 72 British MEPs represent a number of British political parties and never vote as a bloc. The British party with the largest number of MEPs, the Conservatives, has only 25 MEPs, 35% of the total number of British MEPs of 72, and **just over three per cent** of all 736 MEPs.

As and when new countries join the EU, the voting power of the MEPs of each existing member-state is automatically (arithmetically) reduced.

8 **Court of Justice:** The European Court of Justice is superior to the highest national courts of member-states, and in many ways the most powerful of all EU institutions.

- The Commission[9] is the sole enforcer of all EU legislation, with the power to fine member-states for non-compliance.

Information as at February 2011; voting strength as given in The Treaty of Lisbon in Perspective, February 2008, British Data Management Foundation, pages lxviii and lxx.

There are over 30 judges. One of them, Eleanor Sharpston QC, is British. But she, like her fellow-judges, is unable to defend the interests of her own country, or those of any other EU-country: her task is to apply European law. So British voting power is **zero.**

9 **Commission:** See note 3.